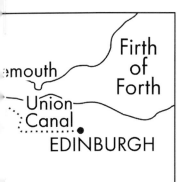

Forth

opened
1790

closed
1963

unlocked 2001

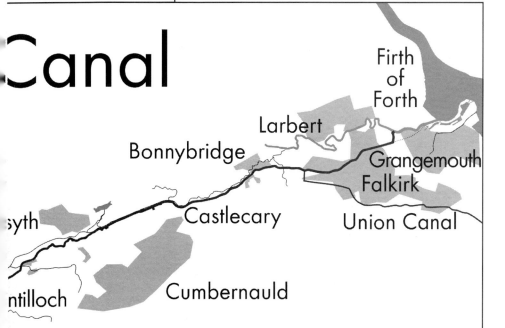

Canal

Firth
of
Forth

Larbert

Bonnybridge

Grangemouth

Falkirk

Castlecary

Union Canal

syth

ntilloch

Cumbernauld

THE FORTH & CLYDE CANAL GUIDEBOOK

PAUL CARTER
Editor

Forth & Clyde Canal Society

Front Cover: *The Forth & Clyde Canal Society's boats in Lock 32, during the celebratory parade to mark the canal's re-opening, 26-28 May 2001.*

First Edition 1985
Second Revised Edition 1991
Third (Millennium) Edition 2001

ISBN 0 904966 52 6

Mapwork by
Lewis Hutton

Published by
East Dunbartonshire Council,
2 West High Street,
Kirkintilloch
G66 1AD
Tel: 0141 776 8090

Printed by
Cordfall Ltd
Glasgow
G21 2QA

Contents

Introduction

What a fantastic weekend on the canal. The sun shone down as a flotilla of forty boats cruised from Grangemouth on the Forth to Bowling on the Clyde. For the first time in nearly forty years, boats were making their way right across the heart of Scotland. Thousands upon thousands of people lined the canal banks, speeches were made, bands played, ribbons were cut, drinks were downed. All to celebrate the reopening of the Forth and Clyde Canal on May 26–28 in 2001.

A 'Fifie' fishing boat from Anstruther and a replica puffer the *Wee Spark* reminded us of the canal's past. The fleet of yachts coming from the Forth sailing clubs and the line up of sleek modern canal barges were harbingers of the canal's future. The flotilla sailed through new and beautifully restored locks and bridges, through busy urban landscapes and through some of central Scotland's most beautiful and peaceful scenery. There were pleasant canal-side pubs to stop at, and plenty of wildlife to see. A particular joy was helming the Forth and Clyde Canal Society's flagship *Gipsy Princess* beneath the infamous A80, the road that closed the canal on 1 January 1963.

The weekend celebration marked the culmination of thirty years campaigning by canal societies, enthusiastic support by canal-side communities, solid backing from local authorities and politicians, and a Herculean effort by British Waterways. Restoring nearly forty locks and building or restoring over twenty bridges plus dredging the entire canal in just over two years was a magnificent achievement. Altogether a sum approaching £80 million has been raised and spent on the entire Millennium Link, renewing and rejoining Central Scotland's two canals, Scotland's two principal cities, and the North Sea with the Atlantic Ocean.

So now we have opened the canal, you have opened this book and our authors will tell you the canal's story. Noted author and Canal Society Chairman Guthrie Hutton starts us off with a lock by lock and bridge by bridge description all the way along the canal, giving details of the many sights to be savoured along the way. Ian Bowman gives details of the canal's fascinating history from construction to eventual closure, taking in early trading craft, steam paddlers, puffers and shipbuilding along the way. Campaign veterans Richard Davies and Donald Mackinnon bring a wealth of personal experience to give us the story of the tremendous thirty-year campaign to reopen the canal. The story of the canal's very full and varied wildlife is brought right up-to-date by Olivia Lassière, British Waterways ecologist for Scotland, drawing on recent wildlife surveys. British Waterways crucial task of looking after the canal has changed dramatically with the restoration of the Millennium Link and their new task is described in a separate chapter. Details of how to enjoy the restored canal are given by myself.

No guidebook would be complete without extensive lists of useful information. These are given in the Appendices. Here you will find lists of all the bridges and locks, boating facilities, historic monuments, road bus and rail links, useful addresses and canal literature. The maps accompanying the chapter 'The Canal Today' show all the main features of the canal and its environment.

Gipsy Princess *passing the crowds at Auchinstarry Bridge on 27 May 2001 during the reopening celebrations.*

The campaign for Scotland's lowland canals does not end with the opening of the Millennium Link. A new chapter in the campaign has opened as well. We need to campaign to involve communities in the canal and to reduce vandalism, to get the right kind of development and to prevent the wrong kind, to ensure British Waterways get proper funding and are properly able to look after our canal heritage. By we, I mean all the individuals and organisations with an interest in our canals and canal-side communities.

I hope you greatly enjoy this *Guidebook* and the canal itself. To increase your enjoyment even more, and help the continued campaign, come and join us, the Forth and Clyde Canal Society.

Paul Carter
Editor
May 2001

Key to map symbols

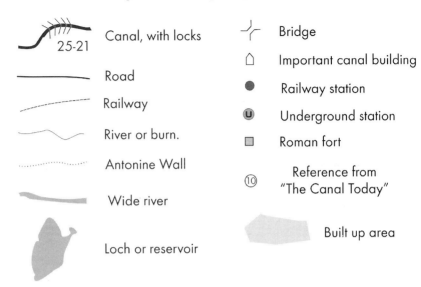

Canal, with locks 25-21		Bridge	
Road		Important canal building	
Railway		Railway station	
River or burn.		Underground station	
Antonine Wall		Roman fort	
Wide river		Reference from "The Canal Today"	
Loch or reservoir		Built up area	

Scale

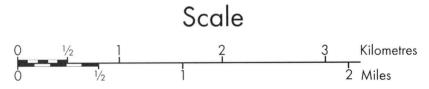

Index of maps

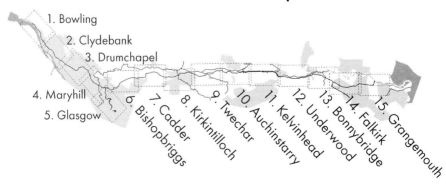

1. Bowling
2. Clydebank
3. Drumchapel
4. Maryhill
5. Glasgow
6. Bishopbriggs
7. Cadder
8. Kirkintilloch
9. Twechar
10. Auchinstarry
11. Kelvinhead
12. Underwood
13. Bonnybridge
14. Falkirk
15. Grangemouth

The Canal Today   Guthrie Hutton

The Forth & Clyde Canal runs from the River Carron, near Grangemouth, to Bowling on the Clyde. It was closed to navigation in 1963 and in succeeding years a number of bridges were replaced by culverts – longer sections were also culverted and filled in. Completion of the Millennium Link project in 2001 has reversed the damage and turned an old canal into a modern waterway. But closure has affected the way the canal looks: as well as the original structures there are many new bridges, locks and other features. These include the project's centrepiece, the magnificent Falkirk Wheel. It is actually on the Union Canal, but sits beside the Forth & Clyde at Carmuirs, and is well worth a visit.

The canal passes through some surprisingly lovely countryside and the greenery continues into some of the country's most populous urban areas. The towpath, lined with trees and edged, in season, with wild flowers also acts as a wildlife corridor for birds and small mammals. The water is home to a rich diversity of plants, insects, animals, birds and fish.

Fishing for pike, perch and roach is a popular canal-side pastime. There are activities on the water too including canoeing, rowing and pleasure boating. Sea going

Bowling Basin.

cruisers, or yachts with their masts stepped, also use the canal. The towpath is ideal for walking, running or cycling, but it is shared by all, and users should try to not inconvenience others. Towpath users should also take care crossing roads at the opening bridges.

This guide starts at the canal's western end – the wind is usually at your back and it reads that way on a map, from left to right. (The numbers in brackets at each stage can be located on the accompanying maps)

1. Bowling

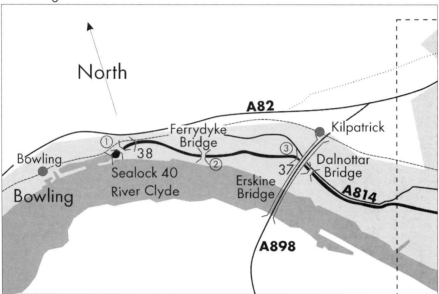

BOWLING [1]

Bowling, with its backdrop of the Kilpatrick Hills and views of the Clyde, is a picturesque spot. Throughout the years when the canal was closed, the locks, bridge and basins here remained open, as a little rump of working canal. It provided fresh water moorings on the Clyde and reminded people what a used canal, busy with boats and people, would be like: Bowling is still busy. The narrow channel between the basins is spanned by a bascule bridge and the impressive, but disused, railway swing bridge. Beside the outer basin is the Customs House, a survival from the days when boats using the canal were engaged in overseas trade. The building is now a British Waterways base. The old sea lock, Lock 39, which gave direct access to and from the Clyde has been disused for many years and boats now enter or leave the canal through Bowling harbour and Lock 40. The railway arches beside the east basin host a number of small businesses. Above Lock 38 the canal water is at its proper, designed level, whereas on most other sections of canal it is lower. This is because the level elsewhere was dropped while the canal was closed, to reduce maintenance costs, and it has not been possible fully to reinstate it. The towpath between Bowling and Clydebank has been incorporated into the Glasgow to Loch Lomond cycle path.

FERRYDYKE BRIDGE [2] 1.09km. (1,190yds)
Ferrydyke Bridge, the first feature east of Bowling, is an original bascule bridge which was restored in the mid 1990s. Beside it is one of the few surviving bridge keeper's cottages. Below towpath level, and therefore easy to miss, are the remains of a stables which, despite their condition, add to an interesting and attractive scene. The Roman Antonine Wall terminated beside the Clyde here and the bridge almost certainly perpetuates the line of the military road that ran behind the wall.

OLD KILPATRICK [3] 1.9km. (1 mile 330yds)
Approaching Old Kilpatrick from Bowling the view is dominated by the Erskine Bridge. It crosses the canal high above Lock 37. The canal heads for the lock round a bend graced by some lovely mature trees. There are access points from the towpath to the 'Saltings' an ecology park set between the canal and river. Just beyond the lock, the Ferry Road swing bridge, which dates from 1934, has been reinstated. It originally carried traffic to the Erskine Ferry, which ceased to operate when the high-level bridge was opened.

DALMUIR WEST [4] 3.86km. (2 miles 700yds)
The bascule bridge at Dalmuir West was, like those at Ferrydyke and Bowling, restored in the mid 1990s as part of an improvement scheme known as the Clydebank Canal Project. The Duntocher Burn passes under the canal through a fine aqueduct close to the bridge.

Dalmuir Bridge, which carries Dumbarton Road over the canal, has undergone many changes. The original bascule bridge was replaced in 1915 by a swing bridge, with rails and overhead cable gantries, so that trams could cross the canal. They did so until only a few months before the canal was closed. After closure the bridge was replaced by a drowned culvert – two submerged pipes built into a solid barrier blocking the canal. In its place is the only drop-lock on a British canal. It is used to lower boats under the road. Towpath users have to cross the road by the traffic lights. Just round the corner from Dalmuir is Trafalgar Street footbridge.

CLYDEBANK SHOPPING CENTRE [5]
The Singer sewing machine factory once occupied a huge site on the offside bank of the canal to the west of Kilbowie Road. The canal here was blocked by a culvert during closure, but it has been opened up under a new bridge. The adjacent Clydebank Shopping Centre offers a wide variety of shops and services. Two footbridges with lifting spans link the two sides of the centre across the canal.

Dalmuir Drop-lock.

2. Clydebank

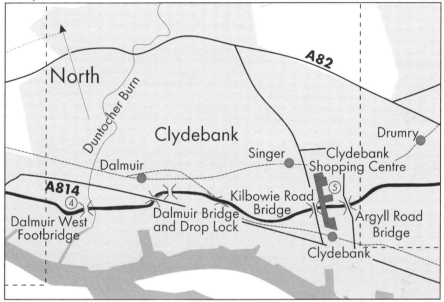

They allow for constant pedestrian access, but boats have to wait while they are raised and lowered. Beyond them, beside the new Argyll Road Bridge, is an unusual kind of ship – it sells fish and chips! To the east, at Linnvale, is another bascule bridge, restored as part of the Millennium Link project.

DUNTREATH AVENUE [6] 8.03km. (4 miles 1,750yds)
The neatly manicured canal banks through Clydebank are the result of a 1970s landscaping project. It ends at Duntreath Avenue, where another new bridge has been built. The road was built after the canal's closure over an extended culvert which included Lock 36. It has been reinstated, with a small footbridge across the tail. There is a lock cottage beside Lock 35. The locks here are part of the Boghouse flight which takes the canal up to Bard Avenue bascule bridge.

Opposite: Gipsy Princess *and* **Janet Telford** *come alongside 'The World's First Sail Thru' Fish and Chip Take Away' at Clydebank.*

3. Drumchapel

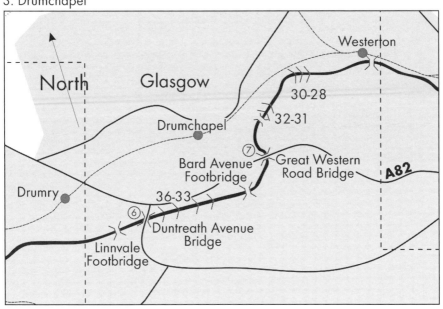

Westerton

North Glasgow

30-28

32-31

Drumchapel

⑦ Great Western
Road Bridge

Bard Avenue
Footbridge

A82

Drumry

36-33

⑥

Duntreath Avenue
Bridge

Linnvale
Footbridge

Restored bascule bridge at Linnvale.

GREAT WESTERN ROAD [7]

The canal bends to the north after Bard Avenue and heads to Great Western Road where new bridges carry the road's two carriageways over the canal. The offside stone abutment from the great lifting bridge, installed in 1930, can be seen under the new bridge decks. The canal was culverted for about 600m. (650 yards) between here and Lock 31, during closure, and reinstatement on the original line was not possible. The footpath therefore follows the old line through the trees, separated for a short distance from the new canal. Path and canal come together again at Lock 32. It has been reinstated, with a footbridge across the tail perpetuating the former line of Blairdardie Road. The road has been re-routed alongside the new section of canal to Great Western Road.

A short pound from the reinstated Lock 31 leads to Cloberhill Locks, Nos 30, 29 and 28. The section from Cloberhill to Temple is spanned by a footbridge at Westerton Station and, at Netherton, by a manually operated swing bridge. The tree clad railway embankment on the offside helps to make this urban section of canal seem almost countrified.

---

canalecdote
A Morris Traveller estate car, stolen in 1975 and dumped in the canal at Netherton with its headlights blazing, was found again when the water was drained for the Millennium Link. A family of coots quickly took up residence on its rusted bonnet.

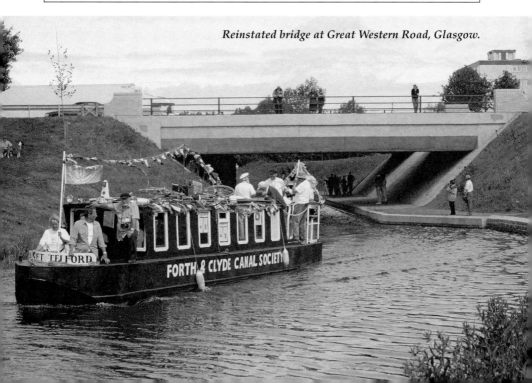

Reinstated bridge at Great Western Road, Glasgow.

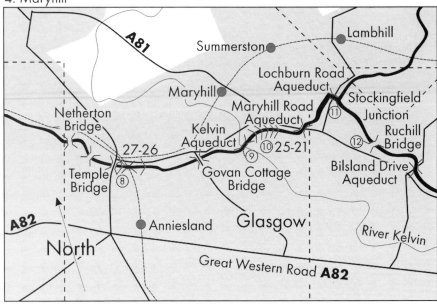

LOCK 27 [8] 12.57km. (7 miles 1,450yds)

A housing scheme at Temple, on the site of an old sawmill, has been linked across the canal by a new bridge. It by-passes the busy Bearsden Road which crosses the canal further to the east on a massive 16.8m. (55ft) span, steel lifting bridge. It was built in 1932 to replace the original Temple Bridge which was a little further to the east across the chamber of Lock 27. The marks of where this was can still be seen on the lock-sides opposite the end of Crow Road North. There are two pub/restaurants here, one which incorporates the old timber-yard offices fronting Bearsden Road, and another on the site of the lock-keeper's cottage. A railway tunnel passes under the canal beside it. Another railway tunnel goes under the canal between Lock 26 and the large gas holders.

KELVIN AQUEDUCT [9] 13.69km. (8 miles 900yds)

Rounding the bends after Temple the canal runs straight for the new Govan Cottage Bridge, at the foot of Cleveden Road. After a short straight run to the east the canal turns to cross the magnificent Kelvin Aqueduct; undoubtedly the finest feature on the canal. It was built between 1787 and 1790 by Robert Whitworth who took over from the original engineer, John Smeaton who retired from the unfinished project in 1775. It consists of four 15.25m. (50ft) arches, with arched spandrels, supported by buttressed piers. The whole structure is 122m. (400ft) long and 21.4m. (70ft) high. When it was completed it was the largest structure of its kind in Britain and so impressed the populace that odes were written in its honour. It continues to impress today and is a scheduled ancient monument.

Although the aqueduct is the finest single feature, the continuous run of masonry that forms the aqueduct and Maryhill Locks, is the finest collective feature on the canal. There is an oval basin between the aqueduct and Lock 25 and similar, irregularly shaped oval basins separate each of the five locks. Beside the basin between Locks 23 and 22 is the dry-dock and slipway of the old Kelvin Dock. This was the oldest boatyard on the canal, opened in 1789. The dry-dock is 44.2m. (145ft) long by 12.2m. (40ft) wide at the top and it descends in steps of dressed stone to a 9.2m. (30ft) wide bottom. It had ordinary lock gates at the entrance and a sluice on one side which emptied the dock through a culvert into one of the lower basins. The boatyard had three berths, one for broadside launching into the dock and two conventional slips for repair or building work.

LOCK 21 [10] 14.21km. (8 miles 1,470yds)

Once past Maryhill top lock, Lock 21, the canal is at its highest point, 47.5m. (156ft) above sea level. The summit reach extends 26km. (16 miles) from here to Lock 20, and also along the Glasgow Branch to Port Dundas.

Maryhill Road passes Lock 21 beside the canal and then, as it heads for the city, drops steeply to go under a great stone aqueduct. It was built in 1881 to replace a smaller original and the canal had to be diverted through a more exaggerated S-bend to go over it. The original aqueduct would have been very similar to the one a short distance to the east, where the canal crosses Lochburn Road. This smaller, more elegant structure was designed by Robert Whitworth a hundred years earlier than the massive bridge at Maryhill Road.

STOCKINGFIELD JUNCTION [11] 15.06km. (9 miles 640yds)

Immediately east of Lochburn Road aqueduct is Stockingfield Junction where the main line heads north and the Glasgow Branch continues east towards the city. The towpath continues along the branch.

(The towpath route along the main line of the canal continues after the description of the Glasgow Branch.)

Lock 21, Maryhill.

The Glasgow Branch

Going on into Glasgow the canal crosses a disused railway tunnel that carried the line north from Maryhill Central to Possil. Alongside it is a 'spillway' or 'waster' which was rebuilt at the time the tunnel was constructed. Spillways are used to control the water level by letting any surplus flow off. This one, with its three arches, stone-lined channel and retaining walls on both sides of the towpath, is one of the most interesting of many such features along the length of the canal. To get the best view of these and other structures, like aqueducts and culverts, it is often necessary to leave the towpath, but care should always be taken when doing this.

The area around Ruchill Bridge was once a hive of chemical-based industries, sited here to keep their polluted emissions away from the city. There was a match factory, rubber works, paint and varnish works, and others, but only one of their fine brick-built buildings survives, to the west of the bridge on the offside. Today's heady aroma emanates from the nearby McDonalds.

RUCHILL STREET BRIDGE [12] 0.64km. (704yds) From Stockingfield Junction Ruchill Street Bridge was reconstructed in the late 1980s as part of a restoration scheme known as the Glasgow Canal Project. The street was realigned so that it could be elevated to clear the canal. In the cut-off end is Ruchill Church with its adjacent hall designed by Charles Rennie MacIntosh.

To the east is Bilsland Drive aqueduct. It was built in 1879 and

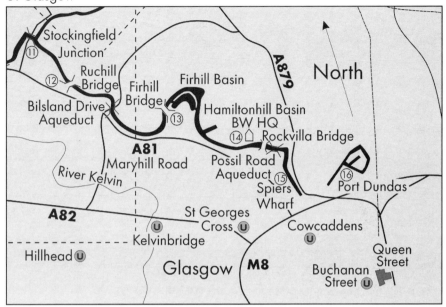

is similar to the one over Maryhill Road, and like it, was made for the expansion of Glasgow's tramway system. On the offside is Glasgow University's student accommodation, Murano Street Village. A footbridge provides access between the village and Maryhill Road.

FIRHILL BRIDGE [13] 1.66km. (1 mile 59yds) From Stockingfield Junction
The canal embankment veers away from Maryhill Road as it approaches Firhill Bridge. This bridge was also reconstructed in the late 1980s as part of the Glasgow Canal Project and given another name – the Nolly Brig. Traditionalists prefer the original!

Beyond the bridge the canal sweeps round a wide bend, with, on its outside, a large timber basin which has silted-up to become a wildlife-rich wetland. It can only be seen from the water. On the inside of the bend is a large kidney-shaped body of water which also used to be a timber basin. It is separated from the main line of canal by an island. The towpath used to run along it until the bridges

---

canalecdote
Children used to gather at Firhill Bridge to greet the 'monkey nut boat' and the crew usually had to let some of the cargo disappear before they were left in peace. The peanuts were destined for a margarine factory at Port Dundas.

---

spanning the basin entrances were removed allowing the island to become a wildlife haven. The footpath now follows the inside of the basin beside Partick Thistle's football stadium, and it rejoins the towpath close to the remains of a stop lock, built during the Second World War to prevent flooding had the canal been bombed. Fine views of the city can be seen from the high embankment east of Firhill. On the offside is a basin cut into a quarry which extracted puddle clay for making the waterproof lining of the canal.

OLD BASIN [14] 2.30km. (1 mile 759yds) From Stockingfield Junction

The embankment continues to the 'Old Basin' at Hamiltonhill, the original terminal of the Glasgow Branch when it reached the city in 1777. The workshop buildings on the offside are still used by British Waterways and the modern office building is their Scottish headquarters. The two storied dwelling house to the rear was used by canal employees until recently. Rockvilla Bridge, the bascule bridge at the east end of the basin, has been restored with hydraulic mechanism.

The Possil Road aqueduct, also built to expand Glasgow's tram system, dates from the 1880s. The original aqueduct, built when the canal was extended in 1790, is still there beside it. Some evidence of the industry that once crowded the area can still be seen to the east of the aqueducts. The causewayed, or cobbled, towpath surface, and the many mooring rings, show how busy with boats and business this area was. There was another timber basin on the offside which,

Ruchill Street Bridge.

like Firhill, was formed by the widening of a sharp bend. It has now been largely reclaimed by the natural world.

SPIERS WHARF [15] 2.89km. (1 mile 1,400yds) From Stockingfield Junction
The towpath skirts around a large electricity pylon opposite the old timber yard; ahead are the Spiers Wharves. At the western end are the remains of another wartime stop-lock. The wharves themselves are wide and impressive, with massive masonry dock walls and cobbled surfaces. Some of the finest mid-nineteenth century industrial buildings in Glasgow survive along Spiers Wharf North. The Wheatsheaf Mills are the most westerly followed by the Port Dundas Sugar Refinery and the City of Glasgow Grain Mills and Stores. Industry last used them as bonded warehouses. They have now been restored as attractive city flats. At the eastern end of the wharf is the old Canal Company Offices, an elegant two-storeyed Georgian building – one of the finest of its period left in Glasgow.

PORT DUNDAS [16] 3.22km. (2 miles) From Stockingfield Junction
The canal appears to stop at the eastern end of the Spiers Wharves, but it does not. The water is culverted and the canal reappears 200m. (220yds) away, across Craighall Road, at the junction of Payne Street and North Canalbank Street. From there it leads into the extensive basins at the former heart of Port Dundas. It was too costly for the Millennium Link project to reconnect the basins with the rest of the canal, so this remains as the ultimate goal; to bring the canal closer to the city centre.
There are many reminders of the basins' industrial past: an old railway swing bridge, a bascule bridge, bollards and crane bases, but the most obvious could easily be overlooked. The huge distillery continues an industry that was established beside the basins when they opened in 1790.
A lot of the water for the Forth & Clyde Canal came through the old Monkland Canal. It ran from Calderbank near Airdrie to the Port Dundas basins and, although it was closed and culverted in the 1960s, a pipeline maintains the water supply.

Stockingfield Junction to Grangemouth

Towpath users wanting to cross the canal at Stockingfield have to go down the ramps leading to Lochburn Road and go through the aqueduct. Care must be taken, however, because the road is narrow and drivers not always considerate!

---

canalecdote
A puffer ran aground beside the mining of village of Lochfauld, near Lambhill, in 1914. She was loaded with household goods and whisky and, while the crew went to get help, the villagers stripped the boat of its cargo in a canalside version of 'Whisky Galore'.

The canal heads north-east from Stockingfield through another wartime stop-lock. A short distance on is a railway aqueduct. Alongside is Hillend Bridge, an aqueduct known unofficially Hallowe'en Pend. It is dog-legged, probably as a result of alterations done when the railway was built. Further on are the remains of an old railway swing bridge.

LAMBHILL BRIDGE [17] 16.69km. (10 miles 660yds) FROM BOWLING

The lifting bridge at Lambhill was built in 1934 to replace the older original. It is now fixed, but provides adequate headroom for boats to pass underneath. Beside it, at street level, is an old stables, one of four built to provide fresh horses at set intervals for the fast passenger boats. They were later used for all canal horses and were known, colloquially, as 'horse barracks'. After Lambhill the city ends almost abruptly, to be replaced by fields and trees, and a distant backdrop of the Campsie Hills.

POSSIL LOCH [18] 17.70km. (11 miles)

Water from Possil Loch flows under the towpath into the canal. The loch and wetland area is home to a variety of birds and has been designated as a site of special scientific interest for its unique plant and insect life. From Possil Loch the canal eases round a long gentle curve and heads due east. Approaching Bishopbriggs, the remains of an old colliery railway bridge protrude from the water like an ancient shipwreck. On the higher ground to the north are the Wilderness Woods.

6. Bishopbriggs

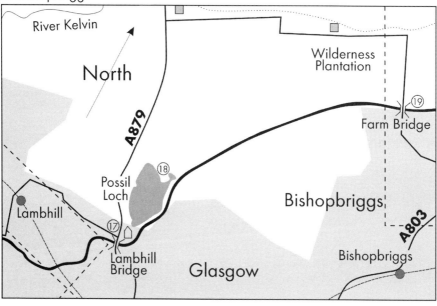

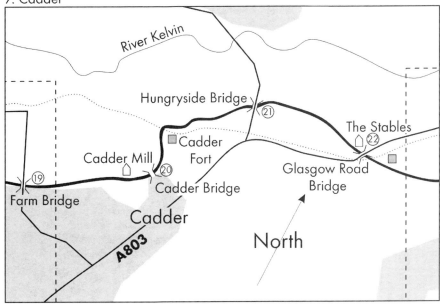

FARM BRIDGE, BISHOPBRIGGS [19] 19.94km. (12 miles 700yds)

Farm Bridge, beside Bishopbriggs Leisuredrome, has been raised as part of the Millennium Link. Throughout the years of closure it was very low and acted as a barrier to large boats between Glasgow and the more attractive sections of canal to the east. Unusually, there is a path on the offside of the canal between here and Cadder. Canal enthusiasts regard the offside as the preserve of wildlife, but this path is sufficiently far from the water's edge to leave the wildlife undisturbed. It affords a different perspective on the canal and a better view of the spillway near Cadder. There is an aqueduct beside it taking a small burn under the canal.

CADDER BRIDGE [20] 21.21km. (13 miles 330yds)

Cadder is one of the prettiest spots on the canal although the original bridge has been replaced by a fixed structure. Adjacent to it, on the towpath side, is a building known as Cadder Mill while

---

canalecdote

Nineteenth century grave robbers, who raided kirkyairds for corpses to sell to anatomy schools, found Cadder kirk an easy target. Its canalside location meant that bodies could be taken to the city by boat. A watchman's hut and iron mort-safe in the kirkyaird show how people tried to stop this.

---

8. Kirkintilloch

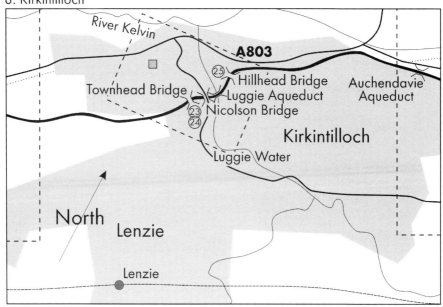

8a. Central Kirkintilloch

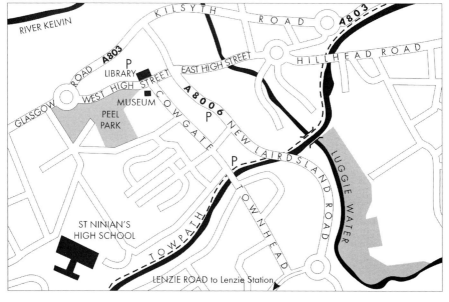

diagonally opposite is the bridge-keeper's cottage with gardens running down to the water's edge. Cadder Kirk can be seen through the trees, a short distance from the canal. The trees also frame distant views of the Campsie Hills and between 1893 and 1939 they provided a romantic screen from the outside world for passengers on the old 'Queen' pleasure steamers.

To the east of Cadder, the canal twists and turns round a series of bends. The sharpest bend cuts through the line of the Roman Empire's Antonine Wall, beside one of its forts. Navvies used stones from the fort to line the canal banks. The high bank to the east of the bend is the rampart of the wall: the canal occupies what was the defensive ditch in front of it.

HUNGRYSIDE BRIDGE [21] 22.48km. (13 miles 1,720yds)

The character of the canal changes again at Hungryside Bridge which carries the Torrance Road over the canal. The bridge, like Lambhill, is fixed, but was built in the 1930s at sufficient height to allow boats to pass through. There is attractive farming country on both sides of the canal between Hungryside and Easter Cadder, where Glasgow Road Bridge crosses the canal.

GLASGOW ROAD BRIDGE [22] 23.76km. (14 miles 1360yds)

Glasgow Road Bridge was a centre for the canal's revival. The Forth & Clyde Canal Society trip boats have operated here for many years. One, an old Clyde passenger ferry renamed *Ferry Queen*, was popular in the 1980s. Her presence along with other boats, required a new slipway to be built on the offside. Much of the activity here was made possible by the presence of the Stables pub/restaurant. It occupies a restored canal stables building, like the one at Lambhill. Glasgow Road Bridge itself was culverted in the 1970s and then rebuilt in the late 1980s as part of the same Glasgow Canal Project, that restored the bridges on the Glasgow Branch.

KIRKINTILLOCH [23]

The canal approaches Kirkintilloch through pleasant rolling countryside. There is a spillway and small aqueduct at the Park Burn, on the town's western edge. Closer to town, on the offside, is a slipway where the boat building and canal carrying firm of J & J Hay used to repair their puffers. Rival boat builders, Peter McGregor & Sons, had their yard in a large basin, which had its entrance at the foot of Hay's slipway. It was originally the transhipment terminal of the Monkland and Kirkintilloch Railway which brought Lanarkshire coal for onward shipping on the canal. The basin has been filled in, but it is still possible to make out where the entrance was. The small arched tunnel below the top end of the slipway is where a feeder lade from the Bothlin Burn enters the canal.

J & J Hay managed to squeeze their boat building yard along the foot of the steep offside embankment to the east of the slipway.

Townhead Bridge, Kirkintilloch.

The Seagull Trust boathouse now occupies part of the site. The Trust is a charitable organisation which provides free canal cruises for disabled people.

TOWNHEAD BRIDGE [24] 26.06km. (16 miles 350yds)

The original wooden Townhead Bridge was replaced by a steel swing bridge in 1933. This was superseded by a drowned culvert when the canal was closed. It looked like an earth dam and acted as a barrier, collecting piles of unsightly, often smelly rubbish. The new bridge has been built on the concrete abutments of the old swing bridge. Because of this the towpath does not go under the road, but rises to street level. Towpath users should take care crossing the busy road.

Kirkintilloch town centre has a wide range of shops, restaurants and other facilities. The canal features strongly in the exhibits at the excellent Auld Kirk Museum. It can be reached by walking north along the High Street from the canal. The nearby William Patrick Library, at the end of the High Street (Cowgate), is also worth a visit. It has a fine collection of canal pictures and reference books.

Nicolson Bridge, to the east of Townhead Bridge, carries the Kirkintilloch by-pass road over the canal. Just beyond it is the Luggie Aqueduct, an imposing single arch topped with fine cast iron railings. The Campsie Branch Railway used the arch in the nineteenth century as a convenient way to cross the canal. They built a culvert over the water as a platform for their tracks. The railway has gone, but now forms part of a walkway which can be reached from the canal-side; it is worth going down to look at the aqueduct from it.

HILLHEAD BRIDGE [25] 26.58km. (16 miles 920yds)
Hillhead Basin, or Kirkintilloch Harbour, was Scotland's first inland port when it opened in 1773; beside it is Hillhead Bridge. The bridge was installed in 1938 and has been reinstated as a working swing bridge.

To the east of Kirkintilloch, the urban area seems to cling on to the canal on the south side while to the north the countryside opens out with splendid views of the Campsie Hills. A small aqueduct takes a minor road under the canal at Auchendavy and a lovely wood rises above the towpath at Shirva Dyke. Opposite is the hamlet of Tintock. To the east, on the offside, are the remains of St Flannan's Colliery, a reminder of the heavy industry that contributed so much to the canal's prosperity. There is a spillway on the towpath side, opposite the old pit.

---

canalecdote

Hillhead basin was a notorious place where the cargoes of unattended coal scows were regularly raided. Women filled their aprons with as much as they could carry and did a runner before the local constabulary could catch them.

Hillhead Bridge, Kirkintilloch.

New hydraulic lifting bridge at Twechar, with British Waterways' boat **The Millennium Link.**

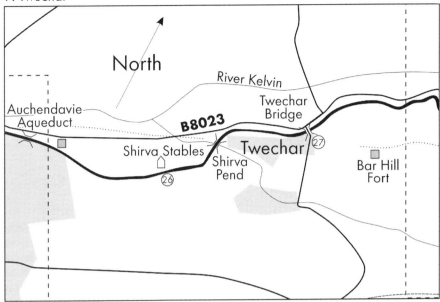

SHIRVA [26] 30.33km. (18 miles 1,500yds)

Shirva is little more than a ruined stables, a farm, and an aqueduct known as Shirva Pend. It is fascinating. Steps lead down to the burn which runs through it on a cobbled base. This also formed a roadway, but there is a raised footpath beside it to keep people's feet dry. East of Shirva the towpath is sandwiched between the road and canal, while on the offside, fields shelve gently into the water. Twechar is on the high ground above them.

TWECHAR BRIDGE [27] 31.51km. (19 miles 1,034yds)

Twechar is a former mining town. One of the few visible reminders of the industry is a derelict mineral railway bridge, to the west of the village. The abutments of the original wooden canal bridge remain alongside the new lifting bridge which was built for the Millennium Link in the year 2000. It replaced one that was installed in 1960, less than three years before the canal closed! To the east of Twechar the towpath remains sandwiched between road and water, but after a

---

canalecdote

'Twechar Beach', a gently shelving field between the village and the canal, was where local children learned to swim. Boys became 'men' when they could swim across the canal and back again with a younger child on their back.

short distance the canal dives away, to twist and turn around the indented base of Bar Hill. Here the canal is at its most lovely with the tree-clad slopes reflected in the dark, sheltered water.

AUCHINSTARRY [28] 34.15km. (21 miles 400yds)

Trees and hill recede at Auchinstarry where the abutments of the old swing bridge guard the cut-off ends of the old road from Kilsyth to Croy. The new road and bridge are a short distance to the east. This was a quarrying and mining community, and to the north is a quarry site that has been turned into a public park. Climbers use it to hone their rock-climbing skills. To the east of the bridge is a large basin where the Forth & Clyde Canal Society based their boat *Gipsy Princess*. She was a vital element in the Society's campaign to preserve the canal environment and bring about ultimate restoration. There is already a good slipway for the launch and retrieval of boats at Auchinstarry and the basin is expected to become the inland equivalent of a marina.

The upper northern and western slopes of Croy Hill are clothed in spoil from Nethercroy Colliery, where many of Auchinstarry's former residents worked. The lower slopes are thickly wooded and quite lovely as the canal winds around them.

CRAIGMARLOCH [29] 36.09km. (22 miles 770yds)

At the north-eastern corner of Croy Hill is Craigmarloch, a spot

10. Auchinstarry

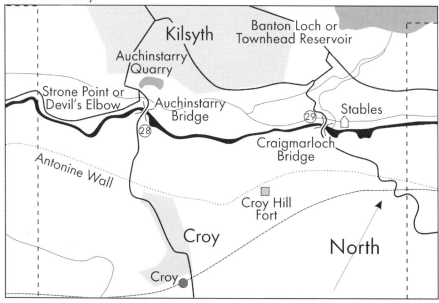

made famous in canal history by the little 'Queen' pleasure steamers that plied the canal between the 1890s and 1939. This was their country terminus; a green haven from city grime. There was a bungalow tea room, a putting green, swings, and a moored barge with tea room and dancing facilities for private parties. It was great! The picturesque location deserves better than the unattractive concrete bridge which replaced an old bascule bridge in the 1980s.

Craigmarloch is a key location for water control, with a spillway to the west of the bridge and, to the east, a feeder lade. When the building of a canal was approved by parliament the use of water within a set distance of it was also sanctioned. The Kilsyth Hills provided a natural source of water above the canal's watershed, and the canal engineers diverted numerous burns into reservoirs to feed the canal. The Craigmarloch feeder flows out of Townhead Reservoir, which is also known as Banton Loch. The canal and its water supplies act as a huge land drainage system, taking millions of gallons, daily, away from flood-prone areas of central Scotland.

Set back from the canal, to the north beside the feeder lade, is another stables building. To the south, is one of best remaining sections of the Antonine Wall. An enjoyable walk can be had which takes in the wall over Croy Hill and Bar Hill and the towpath between Craigmarloch and Twechar.

DULLATUR BOG [30]

To the east of Craigmarloch is a wide, straight section of canal across Dullatur Bog. It was a nightmare to build. The bog kept filling the excavation and thwarting attempts to create a channel. To combat this the engineers drained the bog water into a channel on the north side of the canal and then built up an embankment to carry the towpath, and another on the offside. Over 15.25m. (50ft) of earth and stones were sunk into the bog before the embankments stabilised, and they required constant topping up after that. The canal here is wide and straight and quite different in appearance to the more constrained channel elsewhere. There were a number of small jetties along this stretch and on the offside, at the eastern end of the bog land, is a small side cut which initially served a lime works.

The transition from boggy to solid ground is marked by a change from scrub to mature trees. The canal is also much narrower here and a number of features crowd together. There is a fine masonry spillway and, to its east, a stop-lock – two masonry

---

canalecdote

The navvies digging the summit pound east of Craigmarloch were astonished to find the bodies of men and horses sunk in the Dullatur Bog. They were part of the defeated army who fled from the Battle of Kilsyth in 1645 and were swallowed up by the boggy ground.

11. Kelvinhead

A803

Kelvinhead

Wyndford Lock
Cottage

River Kelvin

Bonny Water

③ ⌂ **Banknock**

30
Dullatur Bog

20
Wyndford
Bridge

Edinburgh & Glasgow Railway

Antonine Wall

North

Cumbernauld

A80

Wyndford Lock with the new bridge on the right.

abutments fitted with gates to close off the canal for maintenance or emergencies.

WYNDFORD LOCK [31] 40.23km. (25 miles 20yds)
Wyndford Lock, Lock 20, marks the eastern end of the canal's summit. There is a small jetty beside it. The restored building on the offside of the lock was a stables-cum-hostelry and the one on the towpath side was the lock-keeper's house. A new bridge has been built below the lock to replace one that used to span the lock. To the east is an attractive tree-lined stretch of canal with a fine aqueduct over the Red Burn.

CASTLECARY BRIDGE [32] 41.50km. (25 miles 1,400yds)
The canal was closed to save the cost of an opening bridge at Castlecary on the A80, Glasgow to Stirling road, then being reconstructed as a dual-carriageway. The new Castlecary Bridge therefore has great symbolic importance for canal enthusiasts. Another, smaller bridge, to the east, has been built to replace the old swing bridge which had remained in position for local access, after being superseded in the 1960s. To the south is the impressive Castlecary railway viaduct.

LOCK 19 [33] 41.99km. (26 miles 180yds)
Three well spaced locks run down to the east of Castlecary Bridge. Locks 19 and 18 are set 460 m. (500yds) apart in open country. An

12. Underwood

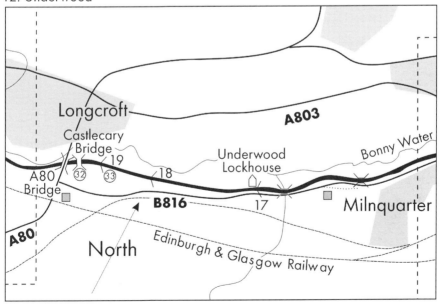

New lifting bridge at Bonnybridge.

inscription on the offside coping stones of Lock 18, under a small footbridge, testifies to its repair in 1817. It required substantial repair again as part of the Millennium Link. Lock 19 at Underwood is 920m. (1,000yds) to the east. Beside it is a lock house and stables building which has been restored as a pub/restaurant. The lockside has been 'causewayed' with rough whinstone cobbles. Underwood is at the western end of what canal men called 'the four mile reach', although it is a bit longer than that. There is one small aqueduct to the east of Underwood and another at Seabegs, to the west of Bonnybridge. There is a fine section of the Antonine Wall here too.

BONNYBRIDGE [34] 42.37km. (28 miles 600yds)

Bonnybridge was a centre for the light iron castings industry, but the canalside foundries have all gone. The bridge here has undergone numerous changes. The swing bridge, which replaced the old bascule bridge in the 1930s, was itself replaced by a culvert which in turn has been superseded by the new lifting bridge. But surviving all is the first bridge, an aqueduct, which is still there just to the east of the new bridge. It is similar to Shirva Pend with running water on a cobbled roadway, and a raised footpath to keep people's feet dry.

The canal heads out into attractive open country after Bonnybridge, with another spillway and small aqueduct at the Rowantree Burn. Carmuirs railway aqueduct marks a change to more urban surroundings, but the structure that dominates the scene is the spectacular Falkirk Wheel.

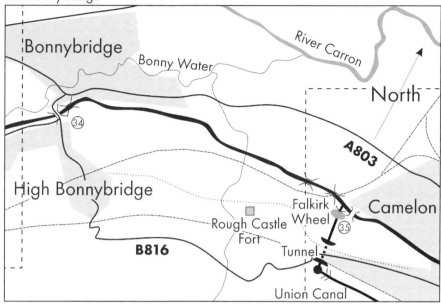

THE FALKIRK WHEEL [35] 48.93km. (30 miles 730yds)

A footbridge gives access across the canal from the towpath to the Wheel. There are on-line moorings for boats and a regulating lock gives access into the holding basin at the foot of the Wheel. The Wheel connects the Forth & Clyde Canal with the Union Canal which has been extended for about 1.4km. (1,500yds) along the south side of the Edinburgh and Glasgow railway. A tunnel, to the south of the Wheel site, brings the Union Canal under the railway and the Antonine Wall, and onto the aqueduct leading to the Wheel. This remarkable structure is the first rotating boat lift in the world, raising and lowering boats 25m. (80ft). There is a visitor centre at its base with a full range of catering and visitor facilities.

LOCK 16 [36] 50.31km. (31 miles 480yds)

The Union Canal's original junction with the Forth & Clyde was a large basin called Port Downie, about 1.5km. (1,600yds) east of the Wheel. The entrance to it can still be seen on the offside just above

---

canalecdote

The Falkirk Wheel is built on the site of an old tar distillery which was burned out in a spectacular fire in 1973. The fire caused massive pollution when tar from ruptured tanks flowed into the canal.

Lock 16.

Lock 16. A crescent shaped flight of eleven locks ran down from the Union to the Forth & Clyde, but they were abandoned in 1933 and filled in. A circular walk, taking in the route of the old locks, the Union Canal extension, the Wheel site and the Forth & Clyde towpath will include virtually every kind of canal feature and be like a canal tour in microcosm. The large pub/restaurant, the Union Inn, was built beside Port Downie as a hostelry for canal travellers. It is better known as 'Auntie Kate's' after a former landlady.

Lock 16 was famous in the canal's heyday because, apart from being at the junction with the Union, it was at the top of the flight of locks up from Grangemouth. It was the terminal for passenger boats from Glasgow and a centre for the iron and chemical industries.

The bridge which used to cross the lock chamber has been rebuilt below it to allow boats an unobstructed passage through the lock. Look for the mason's mark on the new stonework where the old bridge used to be.

LOCKS 16 to 11 [37]

There is a pub/restaurant, the Canal Inn, beside the towpath between Locks 16 and 15. It is probably the canal's oldest pub, predating the Union Inn. Thirteen locks take the canal through Falkirk and between locks 16 and 13 there is a path on both sides. At Lock 14 is an inscription, on a towpath side coping stone, testifying to the repair of the lock in the early 1800s. Lock 11 has been rebuilt above Camelon Bridge as part of the Millennium Link. Beside it, on the towpath side, is a pub/restaurant in a distinctive brick building which was once a bonded warehouse. Diagonally opposite is the Rosebank Distillery with which it was associated.

---

canalecdote

Boys used to get extra pocket money by helping boat crews work up or down Falkirk's lock flight. If they were really lucky, when the boat had reached top or bottom, they would find another going the other way.

CAMELON BRIDGE [38] 51.06km. (31 miles 1,300yds)

The towpath goes under the new Camelon Bridge – a great improvement on pre-Millennium Link traffic dodging. The obsolete Lock 11 is still there beyond the bridge, but boats simply pass straight through it now. There is an old lock-keeper's cottage beside the distillery wall and joist holes in the wall beside Lock 10 indicate where an old canal maintenance depot used to be. There is another old canal cottage beside Lock 9 and the swing bridge which carries the railway line to and from Falkirk Grahamston Station. Lock 8 has been rebuilt to accommodate the new bridge which gives access to the industrial estate on the offside. The remains of the old chamber for Lock 8 can still be seen below the bridge. Lock 7 is just beyond it and Lock 6 about 800m. (880yds) to the east round a sweeping bend.

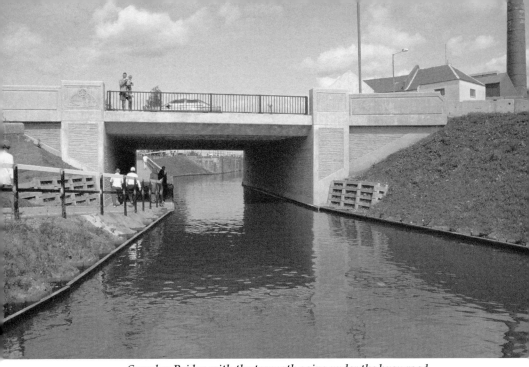

Camelon Bridge with the towpath going under the busy road.

Lock 5 at Bainsford with the old Red Lion pub building behind.

This whole section of canal was once black with iron works, but their dirt and smoke have been replaced by greenery.

BAINSFORD BRIDGE [39] 52.65km. (32 miles 1,280yds)

Lock 5 has been rebuilt upstream of Bainsford Bridge, and the channel lowered for some distance to the old lock chamber, to allow boats clear passage under the reconstructed Bainsford Bridge. The distinctive white-painted building on the towpath side, which is now an antique shop, was once a typical canalside pub known as the Red Lion. The whole of the offside, between the bridge and the obsolete chamber of Lock 5, used to be occupied by the great Falkirk Iron Works, a centre of the light iron castings industry for which the town was famed. Lock 5 also bears inscribed testimony to a repair done in 1816.

LOCK 4 [40] 53.62km. (33 miles 570yds)

The towpath gradually rises on an embankment above the adjacent road until it comes to Lock 4. A pedestrian footbridge crosses the canal to the east of the bridge. It is on the line of a road and culvert which were laid across the canal in 1980. They have now been superseded by the Falkirk Distributor Road which spans the canal on a stylish new bridge a short distance to the east. It has been built on the site of an old railway swing bridge and some of the old structure has been incorporated into the new.

15. Grangemouth

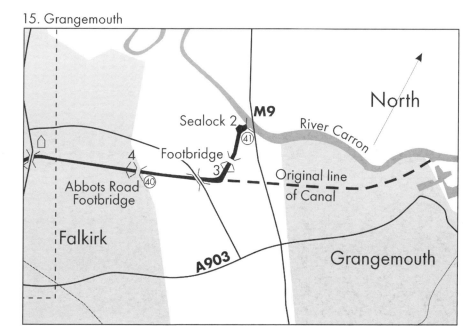

SEA LOCK [41] 55.14km. (34 miles 460yds)

Just to the east of the new bridge was Lock 3, but in the late 1960s the canal was filled in for about 2.4km. (1.5 miles) from it, through Grangemouth, to the sea lock on the River Carron. Although it is still possible to detect the route taken by the canal through Grangemouth, the Millennium Link was not able to reinstate it, and so a new route to the Carron has been created. The old Lock 3 has disappeared and the canal runs directly from the Falkirk Distributor Road bridge into the new channel. It takes a sweeping bend to where a new Lock 3 has been built, with a small footbridge across its tail. Provision has been made for boats to tie up above the sea lock and wait for the right state of tide before heading out into the Carron. Distant views of Fife, on the north side of the Firth of Forth, can be seen above the new sea lock. The lock has been made to the depth of two locks and numbered Lock 2. It gives access to the Carron just up-stream of the bridge carrying the M9 motorway over the river, and is about 1.6km. (1 mile) from its confluence with the Forth.

Navigation on the flowing, tidal Carron River is quite different from sailing on the canal and boaters should consult British Waterways' *Skipper's Guide*, before venturing onto it. As well as the M9, another road bridge and two pipe bridges cross the river, and

The Scottish Fisheries Museum's 'Fifie' yawl, **Whitewing,** *entering the canal through the Carron sea-lock a few days before the grand re-opening of the canal in May 2001. The background digger and foreground scaffolding are part of the transition from construction site to working canal.*

the headroom at these can be tidally restricted. The flat, agricultural carseland to the north of the river is in marked contrast to Grangemouth on the south bank. The old 'Port' used to crowd against this side of the river before the more modern town was built to the east. Large ships were once built on the river banks. Grangemouth Yacht Club is sited beside the old entrance to the canal and the river heads for the sea past the modern docks.

Old Canal

Towpath users cannot follow the Carron because the path ends at Lock 2. The footbridge over Lock 3 leads to the adjacent industrial estate and the road through it leads to the A904 road into Grangemouth. Take care crossing under the M9 bridge at the large roundabout, because traffic is fast and frequent. Follow the A905 going out of Grangemouth for about 500m. (550yds) to Dalgrain Road. Opposite the end of the road, between the A905 and the M9, are two hedges which mark the former banks of the canal. Dalgrain Road has been laid along the bed of the old canal. The old Dalgrain Road ran alongside the old canal and it deviates from the line of the new road where some buildings once fronted onto the canal. The low wall and railing here used to support the towpath. The extensive timber basins are all filled in, although the timber industry still occupies much of the ground. Evidence of the old basin entrances can still be detected in places. At the docks, a road between a large warehouse and a dock basin leads to the Grangemouth Yacht Club and the canal's former junction with the Carron.

History   Ian Bowman

Promoting the Canal

The Forth & Clyde Canal – the Great Canal, as it was called in its early days – was the result of a compromise. Although the idea of making a canal across Central Scotland had been put forward as early as the reign of Charles II, nothing serious was done about it until the middle of the eighteenth century. In the early 1760s the Edinburgh-based Board of Trustees for Fisheries, Manufactures and Improvements in Scotland had surveys made by John Smeaton. The most promising of these envisaged a canal big enough to take seagoing coastal vessels, running from the mouth of the Carron via the valley of the Bonny Water and Dullatur Bog to the valley of the Kelvin and thence into the Clyde at Yoker. The Glasgow merchants opposed the scheme, ostensibly on account of its cost, which was estimated at £78,790, but actually because they were afraid that their trade might be harmed if the canal by-passed Glasgow. They proposed instead a much smaller and cheaper canal, to run from a point on the Carron near the Carron Iron Works to the Clyde at Glasgow. It was estimated that it would cost £40,000. A contest began between the Edinburgh-based promoters of the large canal and the Glasgow-based promoters of the small one.

At first everything went in favour of the Glasgow scheme. By February 1767 £40,000 had been raised and in the following month a Bill for making the small canal was presented to the Commons and reached its second reading before the end of the month. At this point a letter in the press, criticising the scheme for a small canal and commending the proposal for a large one, aroused fresh interest and support for the large canal. There were more letters and articles, even a poem, giving the pros and cons of the case. It was suggested that the small canal would carry goods more cheaply and more frequently than the large one. Against this it was argued that it would require transhipment at each end, with possible long and expensive delays in moving cargoes. Those in favour of the small canal pointed to the success of such inland waterways in England. The protagonists of the large canal maintained that it was not intended as an inland waterway, but was to be a link between two seas. Rivalry between Edinburgh, the capital city, and Glasgow, the centre of commerce and industry, stimulated the controversy. The opponents of the small canal obtained a delay of three months in making the Bill law. John Smeaton was commissioned to make a full survey for a large canal on the lines of what he had already done, but with a cut to Glasgow. It was hoped that this amendment would induce the Glasgow supporters of the small canal to withdraw their Bill, and that is exactly what they did. In December 1767 a Bill for the large canal was introduced, and on 8 March 1768 the royal assent was given to:

> An Act for making and maintaining a navigable cut, or canal, from the firth
> or river Forth, at or near the mouth of the river Carron, in the county of

Stirling, to the firth or river of Clyde, at or near a place called Dalmuirburnfoot, in the county of Dunbarton, and also a collateral cut from the same to the city of Glasgow . . .

In addition, the Act provided for a canal from Borrowstounness [*i.e.* Bo'ness] to the canal entrance on the Carron, but this provision was never carried into effect.

Thus, the compromise brought about between the rival factions by the provision of a cut to Glasgow determined the nature of the canal and earned for it the title of 'The Great Canal'.

A Company of Proprietors of the Forth & Clyde Navigation was set up on 14 March 1768 with the Duke of Queensberry as Chairman. In the following month John Smeaton was appointed Chief Engineer, with Robert Mackell as Sub-Engineer.

Building the Canal

The canal was built from east to west. The first spadeful was dug by Sir Lawrence Dundas on 10 June 1768 at the eastern sea lock. Thence the canal was carried by a series of 16 locks to the village of Camelon, on the outskirts of Falkirk. After a few miles of level running the canal rose by four locks between Underwood and Wyndford to its top level of 47.5m. (156ft) above the sea. It ran at this level right to Stockingfield, on the northern outskirts of Glasgow. The collateral cut was at the same level. From Stockingfield the canal was taken through the lands of Mrs Mary Hill, on the Garbraid Estate. There it began to drop in groups of locks, 19 in all, until it reached the level of the Clyde. The whole construction took 22 years including seven years in which no work was done because of lack of funds.

The first western terminal of the canal was at Hillhead, Kirkintilloch, seen here with pleasure steamer **Fairy Queen** *(1) passing through, c.1895.*

Water was first let into the canal in 1773, when it was filled up as far as Kirkintilloch. For a short while Kirkintilloch was the terminus, until in 1775 the water was taken as far as Stockingfield, which replaced Kirkintilloch as the terminus and soon became a busier port than the Port of Glasgow, on the Clyde. The collateral cut to Glasgow was completed as far as Hamiltonhill in 1777. There a large basin was provided, with wharfage and some sheds. It remained the terminus of the canal for some years, as the Canal Company had run out of funds and the work of construction was stopped. It was restarted in 1784 when the Government approved a loan of £50,000 from the Forfeited Estates Fund to complete the canal. By this time Robert Whitworth had replaced John Smeaton as Chief Engineer. He recommended that the canal be taken to Bowling instead of Dalmuirburnfoot for entry into the Clyde and this was approved. Bowling was reached in 1790. The canal was opened to through navigation in the summer of that year. The first vessel to go through the whole was the sloop *Agnes*, which went from Grangemouth to Bowling on 31 August 1790.

In 1791 the cut to Hamiltonhill was extended to the newly-built village of Port Dundas, adjacent to the Cowcaddens, where wharves and warehouses were provided around capacious basins. Port Dundas then became the main terminus of the canal. In the same year a cut of junction with the Monkland Canal allowed its water supply to be used by the Forth & Clyde. Two years later the locks at Blackhill came into use, enabling the free flow of traffic between the two canals. In 1846 the Monkland Canal was taken over by the Proprietors of the Forth & Clyde Navigation. The canals continued to be managed jointly, in this way, until 1867, when they were purchased by the Caledonian Railway Company to enable railway control of Grangemouth Docks. The Forth & Clyde Canal remained under railway management until 1948, when it was taken over by the British Transport Commission, who had it until 1962 when it passed to the British Waterways Board. Under the terms of the Forth & Clyde Canal (Extinguishment of Rights of Navigation) Act of that year it was closed with effect from 1 January 1963.

The length of the canal from the eastern sea lock to the western one was 59km. (35 miles). The cut to Port Dundas from Stockingfield was 5.6km. (3.5 miles) long, giving a total length of 62km. (38.5 miles). The average width at the surface was 18.3m. (60ft), and at the bottom 9.15m. (30ft). The depth was originally 2.1m. (7ft). It was increased to 2.4m. (8ft) by Robert Whitworth and later to 2.7m. (9ft). The locks were 21m. (70ft) long and 6.1m. (20ft) broad, with a rise of 2.4m. (8ft). The lock gates, made by the Canal Company's carpenters, had paddles raised by cranks or levers. There were 39 locks in all – 20 in the eastern section up to Wyndford and 19 in the western section from Maryhill to Bowling. Many bascule bridges crossed the canal and there were several aqueducts, of which the most notable were those that carried it over the Luggie at Kirkintilloch and the Kelvin at Maryhill. The water in the canal was supplied from 8 feeder reservoirs, the main one being the Townhead Reservoir at Kilsyth.

The work force was recruited mainly from Central Scotland, under a company policy to provide work for local men, particularly the poor and the unemployed. Robert Mackell, the Sub-Engineer, engaged the men and supplied them with spades, shovels and pick-axes. Digging and cutting was done by direct manual labour. Wheelbarrows were used, it is said, for the first time in Central Scotland. Common labourers were normally paid 10*d*. a day. Foremen were paid 'the lowest weekly wage possible'. Workers who sustained injuries were given medical treatment at the Company's expense. The size of the work force fluctuated seasonally. Generally it was in the region of 1000 men, but at harvest time numbers tended to drop. The workers were a tough lot and discipline was hard to maintain, especially as whisky was cheap and plentiful and moral standards were low. Thefts of tools and equipment went on all the time. When the American Revolution began in 1775 half of the work force joined the army. Nevertheless, Mackell somehow managed to get the work done.

During construction most parts of the canal were lined with 'puddle', a thick paste of dampened and compressed clay mixed with gravel or sand. The purpose was to prevent leakage of water. At many places the banks of the canal were revetted with masonry or wood. Dullatur Bog presented special problems and had to be drained by contractors.

Early Canal Trade

The canal served three main purposes. Firstly, and most importantly, it allowed sea-going coastal vessels to pass from one coast to the other without having to undertake the time-consuming and often dangerous voyage round the north of Scotland and without having to undertake any transhipment of cargo. Secondly, it provided a good inland waterway for the movement of agricultural produce, mineral resources and local manufactures across the central belt of Scotland. Thirdly, it acted as a main highway for travellers across Scotland, linking Edinburgh, Perth, Stirling and east coast towns with Glasgow and its surroundings by means of coach services which converged on the canal and connected with the canal boats.

In the eighteenth century the coastal trade of Scotland was carried on by a large number of ships of different types – sloops, smacks, hoys, ketches, brigs and brigantines. These were vessels of from 40 to 80 tons burden, 15m. to 20m. (50 to 65ft) in length, and 4.5m. to 5.5m. (15 to 18ft) in beam. They were bluff-bowed sturdy ships, full forward but tapering somewhat towards the stern with its square counter. They were essentially cargo carriers, with wide, deep holds. Some, however, notably the packet sloops, had accommodation for a few passengers. There was considerable passenger trade up and down the east coast, particularly to London, with regular services from ports in the Forth – Watson's and Kay's vessels from Leith, the Grindley's from Bo'ness, and the ships of the Carron Shipping Company from Carronshore and Grangemouth. The opening of the Basin at Hamiltonhill gave rise to the extension of some of those services through the canal to Glasgow. When the canal was opened right through, passenger services by packet sloops quickly built up between east

The transportation of farm produce was a vital source of income to the Canal Company for many years. The 'cart boat' was one of the services provided to farmers in the 1830s.

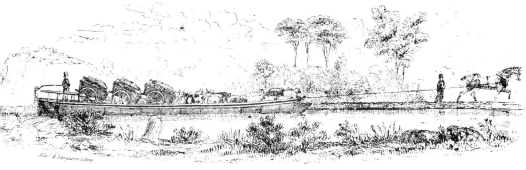

CANAL CART BOAT.

Horse-drawn lighters and scows were the mainstay of the canal cargo service for a long period of time. Some typical vessels are seen here in Grangemouth docks awaiting cargoes for the west.

coast ports – Leith, Dundee, Perth, Montrose and towns on the north-east coast of England – and Liverpool, Dublin and Belfast. The bulk of the sea-going traffic, however, was cargo carrying. Large amounts of grain were brought down from the north-east coast of Scotland and from the Baltic, timber from Scandinavia, various manufactured goods from the east coast of England, and wines, oils and other products from the Continent. From the west coast came tobacco, sugar and textiles, and iron ore from Cumberland. Ships could go through the canal under sail when the wind was favourable, but as a rule they had to rely on horses to 'track' or tow them through. This was a slow process, and as more and more ships began to use the canal there was congestion at each sea lock, where ships had to wait their turn for horses. At the end of the eighteenth century it became so bad that Lord Dundas, Governor of the Company, considered the use of steam tugs to speed things up and commissioned William Symington to carry out steamboat experiments. Between 1801 and 1803 two such boats were tried, the second of which was the famous *Charlotte Dundas*. Back in 1789 Symington had tried out a twin-hulled steamer, the *Experiment*, on the canal. She was the first steamboat to ply on any canal, but no further progress was made at the time. The trials of 1801–3 were successful, but members of the Canal Committee of Management were afraid that the wash from the stern paddles of the steamers would dislodge the puddle which lined much of the banks and placed an interdict on the use of steamboats. Horses continued to tow vessels through the canal right down to the mid-twentieth century.

As well as the sea-going coasters there were numerous vessels for internal use on the canal. These were cargo carriers pure and simple. They had large holds, a small platform at the bow on which the rope could be handled and a slightly larger one at the stern for the helmsman steering by tiller. The smaller boats, in the 12m. to 15m. (40 to 50ft) class, were usually described as scows and were drawn by one horse.

46

The larger ones, 18m. to 20m. (60 to 65ft) long, were classed as lighters and towed by two horses. The distinction between scows and lighters, however, was by no means hard and fast. As a rule these vessels had no mast or cargo-handling equipment, although a few of the lighters had a mast and sails to enable them to be used for estuarial work as well as canal service. The canal scows and lighters had no bulwarks, as these were unnecessary on the quiet waters of the canal and were a hindrance in loading and unloading and in working the locks. However, the Carron Company's lighters were fitted with rails all round. On all of the vessels a narrow gangway ran along the hold on each side. As a rule there were no hatch coamings or covers, although these were sometimes provided on the lighters used for estuarial work.

The scows and lighters handled a variety of cargoes, including coal, sand, limestone, iron ore, pig iron, timber, manufactured goods and agricultural produce. Farmers with land along the canal often found it convenient to have their own scow or scows to move fodder or dung or equipment from one part of their farmland to another, or to take vegetables and other farm produce to markets. From the end of the eighteenth century the Canal Company ran a market boat daily from the eastern sector to Glasgow, and in the 1830s provided 'cart boats' for the accommodation of farmers' carts carrying produce to market, so eliminating the need for the loading and unloading of goods at the canal side. As railway connections with the canal began to develop, the Company brought in 'wagon boats', fitted with rails and a turntable on their decks, which could take on board up to 14 coal trucks direct from the railway. The Canal Company also had a fleet of vessels to assist with canal maintenance, including bank boats, sand & gravel boats, dredgers, ballast boats and ice-breakers. Symington's *Charlotte Dundas* was converted into the Company's first steam dredger in 1811 and worked as such for many years,

Passenger Traffic

Although the canal was primarily intended for the carriage of freight, its potential for passenger traffic was recognised early on. Clearly it could offer a smooth, comfortable means of conveyance. If it was slower than the stage and other coaches, it was considerably safer. The canal had the potential to serve as a central highway connecting Scotland's capital and metropolitan area, in the east, with its growing commercial and industrial centre, in the west. Road services from various places to points along the canal acted as feeders to this central highway.

Passenger services began in 1783 with two 'track boats', the *Glasgow* and the *Lady Charlotte*, which carried goods and passengers daily between Grangemouth and Glasgow, taking the full day for the journey. They were superseded in 1786 by the *Lady Augusta* and the *Lady Catherine*, which were supplemented in 1787 by the *Rose*. In 1809 the Company improved the service by introducing two horse-drawn 'passage boats', the *Charlotte* and the *Margaret*, which carried passengers only and ran between Port Dundas and Lock 16 in five and a half hours. These boats had comfortable stove-heated cabins, with books and games to hand. Meals and drinks were served and a fiddler provided cheerful music. A much-appreciated amenity was a water closet attached to each cabin. At Lock 16 there were coach connections to Edinburgh, Alloa and Kirkcaldy. At Castlecary and later at Wyndford there were coach connections with Stirling, Dunblane, Crieff and Perth. A short-distance coach took passengers from Port Dundas into Glasgow city centre.

By 1816 Henry Bell was operating the *Comet* on the Forth between Newhaven and Grangemouth, connecting there with the passage boats to and from Glasgow and so offering an alternative route between the cities. It proved to be very popular. In 1818 the London, Leith, Edinburgh & Glasgow Shipping Company started an opposition service and soon drove the *Comet* from the route. The Canal Company added the *Morning Star* and the *Thistle* to their fleet of passage boats and in 1819 introduced the *Vulcan*, a passage boat made of iron. She was built by Thomas Wilson at Faskine, on the Monkland Canal, and was the first iron vessel in Scotland. From then onwards iron boats began to take the place of wooden ones on the canal.

In 1822 the Union Canal was joined to the Forth & Clyde at Lock 16, where a basin styled Port Downie was formed, with wharves and sheds and an inn for canal voyagers. It was now possible to travel by canal all the way from Port Dundas in Glasgow to Port Hopetoun in Edinburgh. The Union Canal had its own passage boats, which connected with those of the Forth & Clyde. In 1824 the London, Leith, Edinburgh & Glasgow Shipping Company obtained permission to carry steerage passengers on a night service of track boats they had introduced between Port Dundas and Port Hopetoun. The passengers had to change boats at Port Downie.

During the 1830s the Canal Company sought to cut down running time between Port Dundas and Lock 16 by the introduction of light iron passage boats called 'Swifts'. These were long, sleek, narrow vessels in which some of the previous comfort was sacrificed to speed. They were drawn by two horses, one behind the other, with a postilion on the second one. On straight stretches they could break into a gallop, pulling the boats along at a speed of about nine miles per hour. They reduced the running time between Port Dundas and Lock 16 to three hours. One boat, the *Zephyr*, did the trip in two and three quarter hours. The travelling public were impressed by this speed, and the 'Swifts' were much patronised. The Canal Company invested them with a certain amount of glamour. The skippers were dignified by top hats and cutaway jackets and carried a horn to announce the approach of the vessel. The postilions wore bright uniforms. 'Swifts' has priority of way over all other vessels on the canal, which had to draw in to the bank to let them pass. They came up to the wharves at the ports of call at full gallop, with the skipper sounding his horn. Some experiments were made in running 'Swifts' right through to Port Hopetoun but were not followed up. The 'Swifts' ran as far as Lock 16, where passengers transferred to similar boats on the Union Canal. Light iron pasage boats, however, were soon introduced to the night service and ran through without change. They were popularly known as 'Hoolets', a name analogous with 'Swifts' and derived from the sound of their horns during the night, which was reminiscent of the hooting of owls. An interesting feature of both 'Swifts' and 'Hoolets' was the provision of headlights for night running. These were polyphotal lamps, designed by John Scott Russell, in which reflectors were used to throw a wide neam of light from oil burners in front of the boat, to shine on the towpath as well as on the water.

In the two decades of their existence the 'Swifts' built up a legend that lived long after they had vanished from the canal. When the Edinburgh & Glasgow Railway was opened in 1842 it provided formidable competition, later reinforced by the alternative route of the Caledonian Railway Company. The Canal Company was unable to stand up to this competition and decided to relinquish their passenger service. Its service of 'Swifts' was discontinued with effect from 11 March 1848. For the next three years a private company, A. & J. Taylor, ran one 'Swift' between Port

Dundas and Lock 20, at Wyndford. In 1852 this firm was allowed to extend its service to Lock 16, employing two 'Swifts'. In 1860 they modernised the service by introducing a screw steamer, the *Rockvilla Castle* (also often referred to as the 'Swift'). This little vessel, with her jaunty red funnel amidships, gave a useful service to villages along the canal. When the Taylors went out of business in 1875 she was taken over by George Aitken, a Kirkintilloch man, who employed her on general service and for pleasure cruising between Port Dundas and Craigmarloch. She captured the fancy of the public and her cruises were very popular. George Aitken was drowned in a tragic accident at Cadder in 1880 and the *Rockvilla Castle* was withdrawn and broken up in the following year. In 1893 Aitken's son, James, revived the cruising with a small single-screw steamer called the *Fairy Queen*, and so popular did it become that by 1906 he had three steamers plying between Port Dundas and Craigmarloch, with occasional trips as far as Lock 16. The three steamers were the *Fairy Queen* (2), the *May Queen* and the *Gipsy Queen*, the first *Fairy Queen* having been sold to Ireland. The two *Fairy Queens* carried on the red funnel tradition of the *Rockvilla Castle*, but with the advent of the *May Queen* in 1903 a new livery was adopted – a yellow funnel with white hull and upper-works. Carrying this livery the little steamers had a yacht-like appearance

*The **May Queen** of 1903 was built at Kirkintilloch,*
the only pleasure steamer to be built beside the canal.

Gipsy Queen, *here at Craigmarloch, was the best known of all canal pleasure steamers.*

and graced the canal for many years. The last one in service, the *Gipsy Queen*, was withdrawn in 1939, just after the start of the Second World War, but their memory lives on in the affections of those who knew them, and of many to whom they are only names.

The Steam Paddlers

The use of steamers on the canal has an interesting history. Reference has already been made to William Symington's work with the twin-hulled paddler *Experiment* in 1789, which gave the Forth & Clyde the distinction of being the first canal in the world to carry a steamboat on its waters. His later experiments with two stern-paddle tugs, in 1801–3, demonstrated the real potential of what might be achieved. The second boat, the *Charlotte Dundas*, was well ahead of her time in the design of her engine, with a horizontal cylinder giving direct drive to the paddle wheel. The unfortunate decision to stop her plying as a tug and to ban the use of steamboats on the canal lost the Company the opportunity of being in the forefront of steam propulsion. During the next quarter century, while steamboat services were proliferating on the Clyde and the Forth, the canal that connected them was still using horses as motive power. In 1828 Thomas Grahame, an enterprising member of the Canal Company and a steam engine enthusiast, hired a small paddle steamer, the *Cupid*, from David Napier and

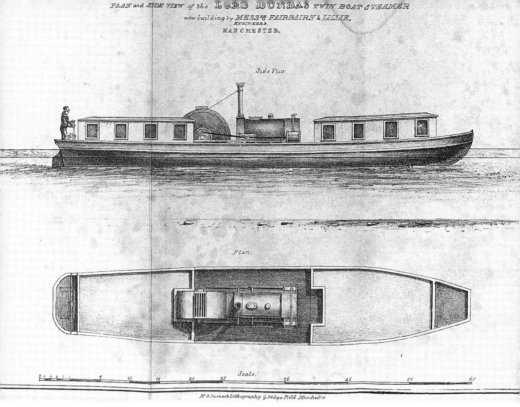

Side View.

Plan.

Scale.

*Lord Dundas was built in Manchester in 1831, as part of a serious drive
to introduce steam navigation onto the canal at that time.*

demonstrated that she could tow passage boats more cheaply and efficiently than horses at five miles an hour, with no damage to the canal banks. The ban on the use of steamboats was then lifted.

In 1829 the Company handed over an iron passage boat called the *Cyclops* to John Neilson at Hamiltonhill, to be fitted with a steam engine and stern paddle similar to those used on the *Charlotte Dundas*. She ran for almost a decade between Port Dundas and Alloa, carrying goods and occasional passengers. In 1831 the Manchester firm, Fairbairn & Lillie, built a light iron twin-hulled paddle steamer for the Canal Company. She was called the *Lord Dundas*. They sent her by canal to the Mersey, up the coast to the Clyde and along the Forth & Clyde to Tophill, Falkirk, for trials. She was said to be the first iron vessel to sail on the open sea. She had a 2-cylinder engine, of 10 horse power, set amidships, with direct drive to a single paddle wheel placed between the hulls just aft of the engine. After a couple of years in which she was used mainly as a tug for passage boats, she was converted for use in an experiment in which a chain was laid along the bottom of a section of canal, and was led over a wheel between her hulls which pulled her along as it turned. The experiment was unsuccessful. In 1836 the *Lord Dundas* had her engine removed and was turned into a barrack boat for canal workers. The *Manchester*, also built by Fairbairn & Lillie, came onto the canal in 1832. She was an improved version of the *Cyclops* and ran on the goods service between Port Dundas and Stirling until 1837. Another steamer of 1832

51

was the *Edinburgh*, built by Thomas Wilson at Tophill. Wilson, the builder of the *Vulcan*, had been transferred to Tophill as resident Engineer. The *Edinburgh* was put onto the night service between Port Dundas and Port Hopetoun. However, she was found to be unsuitable for use on the Union Canal and after a few months was withdrawn and converted into a tug for use in Grangemouth Harbour, where she gave good service for many years. In 1836 John Neilson built the *Vesta*, a paddle tug, for the Canal Company. She was probably the most successful of the steamers of the 1830s and brought considerable income to the Company from her towing. At the end of the decade only she and the *Edinburgh* were still running as steamers.

During the early 1840s the Canal Company conducted experiments with screw propulsion in an iron light passage boat fitted with a steam engine, but these were not followed up. A new group of paddle steamers appeared on the canal – the *Prince of Wales* and the *Experiment*, which were probably 'packet tugs' running between Port Dundas and Greenock – and the *Gipsy*, a very small undecked paddler which achieved fame in 1843 when she was sold for duty on Loch Katrine and became the first steamboat to ply on the loch. She was bitterly opposed by the local boatmen and disappeared mysteriously one night. A farmer returning from Stirling in the early hours of the morning claimed to have seen her sinking in the deepest part of the loch, but the mystery of how she got there was never solved. In 1845 the Canal Company placed the *Firefly* on the canal. She was driven by Kibble's Patent Propeller, an arrangement in which an endless belt with floats on it ran over two wheels on each side of the boat and drove her along. She was used successfully to tow light iron passage boats. However, when the 'Swifts' were discontinued in 1848 she had her engine and propelling machinery removed and was used as a pay boat. In 1850 the Carron Company acquired a small paddler called the *Rob Roy*, their first steamship. They used her to tow lighters on the top level of the canal until 1870, when she was broken up.

Puffers

Thus far, the emphasis in steam propulsion had been on paddle steamers used as tugs. In 1856, however, there was an important development arising from the experiments with screw propulsion in the 1840s. James Milne, the Canal Company's Resident Engineer at Hamiltonhill, fitted a 2-cylinder steam engine driving a single screw into the Company's iron lighter *Thomas*. Her trials on the stretch of canal between Stockingfield and Bowling were most satisfactory, and the owners of lighters and scows quickly realised that here might be the answer to their towing problems. Before long many of the horse-drawn lighters had been fitted with steam engines driving screws, ushering in a new era on the canal. At the end of 1857 the Swan Brothers at Kelvin Dock (Maryhill) launched the first purpose-built screw lighter, the *Glasgow*. She is generally accepted as the progenitor of the race of puffers that became such a feature of the canal, and of the estuaries of Clyde and Forth. In the early boats the exhaust was turned up through the funnel to help draughting. This produced a puffing noise that earned for the boats the name of 'puffer' – which continued to stick long after more sophisticated machinery had done away with the puffing. In all, some 400 puffers were built. All were single screw vessels, with engine and funnel set well aft. With a very few exceptions, such as the *Joanna* of 1858, they were made of iron or steel.

The first puffers were designed on the lines of canal lighters. They were flush-decked, with little or no sheer, and had no bulwarks or hatch coamings. Steering was by tiller, as in the horse-drawn lighters. As steam was available to drive a winch, they were usually fitted with a mast and derrick well forward. These boats were for use only on the Forth & Clyde and Monkland canals, and were known as 'canal screws' or 'inside boats'. Some of the owners, however, such as the Hay brothers, the Burrells, the Salvesens and the Carron Company, were involved in coastal as well as canal trade. This led to the development, from the 1870s onwards, of a sea-going type of puffer, based partly on the canal vessels and partly on the coastal sailing vessels it was designed to replace. There was more freeboard in the hull, which had bulwarks all round and considerable sheer fore and aft. The boats were bluff-bowed, but had good curves in the run under water, The hull was round-bilged and strengthened by a bar keel, for the boats often had to be beached to unload cargoes. By the 1890s a raised quarter deck was usual. It gave greater buoyancy and more bunker space. The sea-going boats had wheel steering of the chain and barrel type. Under Board of Trade regulations they had to have hatch coamings and covers, link bars, load lines. They were called 'outside boats' in contrast to the internal canal vessels, which were 'inside boats'. An intermediate type of vessel was the 'shorehead boat', so called because it was developed to operate within the shorehead limits of the Firth of Clyde, from Skipness to Garroch Head. These boats were like the outside boats in general design, but were slightly smaller and carried a crew of three, as compared with the four men who made up the crew of an outside boat. Shorehead boats were not required to have bulwarks, hatch coamings & covers or any of the other equipment required by seagoing vessels. However, most were provided with them.

Shipbuilding on the Canal

As all of the nineteenth century puffers used the Forth & Clyde Canal, their dimensions were limited by the size of the locks. Most of them were built in yards along the canal. Shipbuilding was probably the first industry to be attracted to the canal side. The earliest recorded builder was James Welsh, who was building sloops and lighters at the eastern sea lock in the 1780s. During the next decade the Canal Company provided carpenter's yards with graving docks for repairing and building vessels at Tophill, Falkirk; Kelvin Dock, Maryhill; and Bowling. At the Hamiltonhill Basin in Glasgow there was a carpenter's yard with a slipdock. The yard at Tophill was used for the Canal Company's vessels only, but at the other yards the ship carpenter in charge was encouraged to take orders from other shipowners and considerable building took place, particularly at Kelvin Dock. During the early years of the nineteenth century Richard Bowden had a boatyard in the Timber Basin at Grangemouth, and in the latter part of the century William Drake was building lighters, fishing boats and steam launches on the other side of the Basin. He was followed by David McGill, who built and repaired lighters. McGill had a slipway, with a trolley to bring the boats out of the water. During the 1820s Alexander Sclanders, who had been helmsman on the *Charlotte Dundas*, had a small boatyard at Lock 16. It was later used by Thomas Wilson, builder of the *Vulcan*. Wilson's son, Robert, started a small shipyard at Port Downie and built some good sloops as well as canal vessels. During the 1850s this yard was taken over briefly by Thomas B. Adamson, a Grangemouth shipbuilder, and from him it passed to one of his

A typical broadside launch at Kirkintilloch:
the **Serb** *enters the canal with a splash on 23 September 1927.*

employees, Gilbert Wilkie, who played an important part in the development of the outside puffer.

Towards the end of the 1860s James and John Hay took over a small yard at Kirkintilloch and built some of the best known and most successful puffers on record. Their yard built the *Saxon* (ex-*Dane*) which featured in one of the television series about Para Handy. From the yard also came the *Boer* and the *Inca*, stars of the film 'The Maggie', and the *Kaffir*, which appeared in a film about the Loch Ness Monster. Another Kirkintilloch yard was that of Peter McGregor, a local timber merchant. He started building vessels at the Railway Basin at the beginning of the twentieth century and produced a variety of vessels, including the first 'motor puffers'. Some of the ships he built were too big to go through the canal locks and were sent in sections to Bowling for assembly, giving rise to the remark that McGregor built the longest ships in the world, for when the bow was in Bowling the stern was in Kirkintilloch! Both the Hays and Peter McGregor launched their vessels broadside on.

In the Hamiltonhill area there was considerable shipbuilding activity. During the 1830s John Neilson built several paddle steamers in the yard at the basin. In the next decade Yule & Wilkie at Springbank and Napier & Crichton at the Canal Basin built iron lighters and schooners. Between 1875 and 1903 Burrell & Son had a yard at the Clay Cut, where they built many puffers, both for their own use and for other owners. In 1843 the Canal Company installed one of Morton's Patent Slip Docks in one of the basins at Port Dundas. It was available both for its own vessels and for those of other owners. William Jack & Co. built some puffers there during the early years of the twentieth century.

Kelvin Dock has already been mentioned as the birthplace of the puffer. Its building record goes back to the 1790s and a great variety of vessels came from its slips, some being launched broadside, others end on. Various ship carpenters held the lease of the yard. The longest tenure was by the Swan family, who held it from 1837 until 1893 and served a wide circle of customers, including some from overseas. It was the Swans who first developed the building of vessels in sections on the canal. They also built at the yard at Blackhill, on the Monkland Canal, later taken over by the Cumming family. The last launch at Kelvin Dock was in 1921, although the yard remained in use until 1949. Shipbuilding in the Canal Company's yard at Bowling had terminated during the middle years of the nineteenth century, when alterations to the basin at the sea lock required its closure. The McGill family had built most of the ships launched from this yard, and when it closed they joined with the Scotts to form a yard in Bowling Bay. This remained in production for many years and its output included the 'Anzac/Lascar' puffer type of 1939, which became the prototype for government 'VIC' boats during World War II. During the 1860s R.S. Ferguson had a small yard at Firhill, where he built wooden schooners and lighters, but it did not survive beyond the end of that decade.

Canalside Industries & Canal Cargoes

The Forth & Clyde Canal, running as it did through a part of Scotland rich in mineral resources, offered facilities for the transport of raw materials and manufactures and for the supply of water for steam engines in factories. The records of the canal testify to the development of industries along its banks – foundries and iron works, engineering plants, distilleries, factories of various types. The foundries were early in the field, from Bainsford to Hamiltonhill and Port Dundas. Engineering shops were not long behind them. Hugh and Robert Baird, sons of Nicol Baird, the Canal Surveyor, had an engineering shop at Hamiltonhill before 1800. John Neilson was their neighbour at Oakbank, with a foundry and engineering business. During the nineteenth century numerous foundries and engineering works were established along the Canal – Burnbank Foundry at Bainsford, Peter Taylor's engineering workshops at Falkirk, Port Downie Iron Works, Smith & Wellstood at Bonnybridge, the South Bank, Lion and Basin foundries at Kirkintilloch, the Lambhill Forge and Foundry, the Lochburn Iron Works at Possil, Firhill Iron Works, Yule & Wilkie at Springbank, the Caledonia Foundry, the Maryhill Iron Works and others.

Foundry workers lost a great deal of liquid content from their bodies in the course of their work and were often given beer to make it up. Hugh and Robert Baird even acquired a brewery at Hamiltonhill and developed it alongside their foundry and engineering works, later expanding into malting and distilling. An important cargo on the canal was grain for local distilleries, brought down from the north-east of Scotland and from the Baltic and sent through to the west. Not surprisingly, distilleries were established at various places along the canal – Rosebank Distillery at Falkirk, Bankier Distillery at Wyndford, Port Dundas Distillery in Glasgow, and others, right down to Bowling. Some fine malts and blended whiskies were produced on the canal banks – though not from the canal water!

The development of coal mining in Central Scotland was greatly assisted by the canal, which provided a convenient means of moving coal in bulk eastwards to Grangemouth, for export to the Continent, or westwards to the Clyde, for use in the industrial West of Scotland or for export to Ireland or farther afield. Some collieries, such as Bairds' at Twechar or the Gardners' at Meiklehill, Kirkintilloch, had their own 'couper', or loading point, on the canal, where lighters were brought alongside to take on coal. Canalside collieries also supplied fuel to foundries, works and factories along the canal.

The canal had a close and important connection with the timber trade. Large consignments of timber were brought to Grangemouth from Scandinavian and Baltic countries, and, at one period, from Canada. The Canal Company provided extensive timber basins at Grangemouth, at Kirkintilloch, at Firhill and at Port Dundas. There were small timber ponds at Maryhill Locks, at Temple and at Bowling. Timber businesses soon developed around them: Brownlee and Muirhead at Grangemouth and Glasgow; Peter McGregor at the Railway Basin in Kirkintilloch; the Swans at Kelvin Dock; and many others. Numerous sawmills operated on the banks of the canal, from one end of it to the other, and drew water from it for their steam engines. They included St John's Sawmills at Grangemouth, Bonnybank Sawmills at Bonnybridge, McGregor's Sawmill at Kirkintilloch, the City Sawmills and Rockvilla Sawmills at Port Dundas, Ruchill Sawmills, the Western Sawmills at Firhill, and the Temple Sawmills at Anniesland.

Timber from Grangemouth Docks to sawmills in the west of Scotland,
was one of the most common canal cargoes. Here the puffer **Gael** *is seen moving*
west through Craigmarloch Bridge with a load of timber in the late 1930s
(photograph by the late John Watson, Kilsyth).

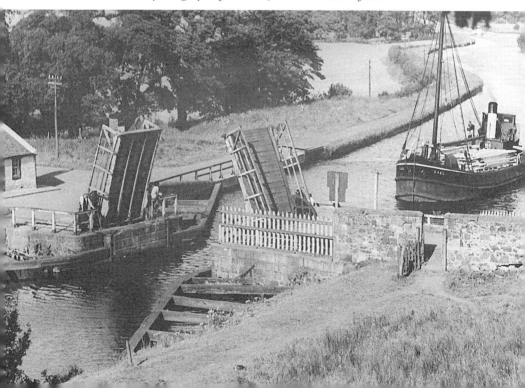

The Kelvin Valley was rich in sand deposits from bygone seas. Sand-pits were worked adjacent to the canal, and there was a good deal of quarrying also, with convenient transport available in the canal lighters. The availability of both sand and coal supplies along the canal led to the development of a glass industry, mainly in the Glasgow area, with the Victoria Glass Works at Hamiltonhill, the Glasgow Glass Works not far away, and the Firhill Glass Bottle Works and Forth Glass Works at Firhill. A range of chemical works were also established on the canal banks, including Ross's Chemical Works and Scottish Tar Distillers at Camelon, the Paraffin Works at Stockingfield, the Phoenix Chemical Works at Firhill, the Port Dundas Chemical Works and the Kelvindock Chemical Works. The transport facilities of the canal were the main reason for the establishment of a nickel smelter at Kirkintilloch by the New Caledonia Mines Company. The areas of industrial growth at Grangemouth, Falkirk, Kirkintilloch and Glasgow contrasted strikingly with the pleasant rural sections of the canal in between. For almost two centuries of working life the canal carried a variety of cargoes – bulk cargoes, such as coal, pig iron, sand, grain, timber, limestone; and packaged cargoes of manufactured goods and casks of oil and wine. Perhaps the strangest cargo carried by vessels going through the canal consisted of consignments of large casks labelled 'bitter salts', with an Edinburgh address. They were sent from Liverpool to Leith in the mid-1820s, in sloops of the Carron Line running through the canal. A chance opening of one of the casks during loading at Liverpool revealed that they contained human bodies, obviously intended for the Edinburgh anatomy tables!

From the Old Era into the New

During its commercial lifetime the canal witnessed some unusual vessels on its waters, from Symington's twin-hulled paddler *Experiment* of 1789 right down to June 1952, when canal-side residents were alerted to the presence of a submarine in its waters. This was the midget submarine XE IX, commanded by Lt W. Ricketts, on her journey from Clyde to Forth. She came through at walking pace and stopped overnight at Kirkintilloch, where she was moored at Hays' boatyard. The passage of XE IX served as a reminder that some of the earliest enthusiasts for a cross-Scotland canal had seen its main purpose as a strategic route for warships. In 1952 closure was still a decade away, but traffic on the canal was gradually slowing down. Many of the canalside industries had moved elsewhere or had closed, and the fleet of puffers was being steadily reduced. The last horse-drawn lighters had recently vanished, but fishing vessels and yachts still used the canal as a convenient route across Scotland, if less frequently than in earlier years. The last passenger trip was on 12–13 October 1962, when the Motor Vessel *Ashton* sailed on a charter from Bowling to Kirkintilloch and back. A few weeks later some fishing boats were the last vessels to go through the canal, before its official closure.

In 1948 the canal had been taken over by the British Transport Commission. It was no longer a profit-making concern and for many years there was discussion over its future. Control of the canal passed to the British Waterways Board, under the terms of the Transport Act of 1962. That year the Forth & Clyde Canal (Extinguishment of Rights of Navigation) Act was passed. It came into force on 1 January 1963, curtailing all traffic on the canal, with immediate effect. This enabled the A80 Glasgow–Stirling road, then being improved, to cross the canal at a low level. The needs of road

The bridge on the main road at Castlecary caused many problems over the years. The bascule bridge, shown here, was one of the first on the canal to be replaced by a steel structure to meet the needs of main road traffic in 1927. The replacement bridge in turn proved inadequate and improvements to the road at Castlecary was the stated reason for the closure of the canal on 1 January 1963.

development had been a major factor in bringing about the canal's closure. During the 1960s parts of the canal were sold or otherwise disposed of to local bodies and infilling began to take place at various localities. The timber basins at Grangemouth and the canal from the eastern sea lock to Lock 3 were filled in. A road was built on the alignment of the canal for much of the way up to Lock 3. There was infilling at Bainsford Bridge and at Camelon, to enable the Glasgow road to be widened and a bottleneck improved. In 1967 the swing bridge at Townhead, Kirkintilloch, was replaced by a broad modern structure, built on an embankment that blocked the canal. In 1975 the Glasgow Road Bridge, on the A803 west of Kirkintilloch, was superseded by an embankment and low culvert, with very little headroom. At Port Dundas the timber basin was infilled in 1967 and most of the basins beyond North Spiers Wharf were covered over during the mid-1970s. During the late 1960s and early 1970s infillings were made at Ruchill, Cleveden Road, Cloberhill (Locks 31 & 32) and Duntreath Avenue (Lock 36 and loading pier). There was a blockage at Kilbowie Road, Clydebank, for pipes, from 1968, and infilling at the swing bridge on Dumbarton Road, at Dalmuir. Pipe crossings at various other places along the canal caused blockages also.

The modern revival of the canal is now a matter of historical record. Groups of enthusiasts began to draw attention to its potential as a leisure amenity. Over the last three decades of the twentieth century their campaigns gathered ever-increasing momentum. Power-boat rallies and canal-side festivals served to demonstrate the possibilities that clearly existed. Trip boats were introduced during the early 1980s, although then restricted to short-distance travel. Soon afterwards the 'minimum 3 m.

(10ft) clearance' rule was introduced for all new bridges over the canal. After some initial disappointment, the Millennium Link scheme achieved the necessary £78m funding and construction work was inaugurated by the late Donald Dewar on 12 March 1999. The early years of the twenty-first century will witness one of the most spectacular revivals in the history of public transport. Phoenix has arisen from the ashes.

This chapter has been revised for this Guidebook *although it remains substantially as written for the first edition by the late Ian Bowman. Ian was a great authority on the canal, writing a number of books on its history and the vessels that sailed on it. His death, soon after the publication of* The Gipsy o' Kirky *in the year 1987, robbed us all of a true gentleman, and perhaps more books to add to the priceless legacy of historical research he left.*

The drowned culvert at Kirkintilloch Townhead was an eyesore for over 30 years before being replaced by a new bridge in 2000 as part of the Millennium Link project.

Campaigning for Restoration
Richard Davies & Donald Mackinnon

Richard Davies was the voluntary working party organiser for the Scottish Inland Waterways Association during the 1970s. He became secretary of the Forth & Clyde Canal Society during its formative days, and was later elected chairman.

Introduction

During the years of neglect following closure on 1 January 1963, the Forth & Clyde Canal had fallen into an appalling state. There were few memories of the canal's more picturesque past — only a fear and loathing of the 'Gutter Canal' fuelled by its bad press. Throughout the sixties and early seventies the 'Killer Canal' headlines were reinforced by politicians' assurances that the canal would be filled in as soon as money was available. It was not just a derelict canal that had to be restored; we would first have to restore its image.

A tea-party in the chamber of Lock 21, Maryhill,
to celebrate its newly cleaned up status in 1976 (picture: Douglas Johnston).

This chapter tells how the canal managed to lose the name that one newspaper gave it — the 'Filth and Slime Canal'.

Face-lifting the Canal

The Scottish Inland Waterways Association (SIWA) was founded in May 1971 and aimed to promote both the conservation and restoration of all Scotland's canals and waterways. In the same year the Scottish Civic Trust had launched its 'Face-lift Glasgow' campaign. This encouraged the Glasgow Students' Charities Appeal to hold a sponsored clean-up of the Forth & Clyde Canal at Temple and Maryhill where 200 students removed 1000 tons of rubbish in a weekend. The new Scottish Inland Waterways Association, now augmented by some of the Glasgow enthusiasts, began a series of voluntary working parties. But it was not long before attention was diverted by the tragic drowning of four small boys at Clydebank in 1972 resulting in a call for the elimination of the canal. Now, however, for the first time, and as a result of the clean-up activity, a debate began on the question of whether a derelict or a restored canal was safer. The safety question led to the canal in Clydebank being shallowed, but still with about 1m. (3ft) of water, sufficient in engineering terms for the water flow.

The Need for a Plan

In 1973 the Strathkelvin Canal Park Group (SCaPa) launched their idea of a country park based on the canal. This idea, when added to the urban face-lift activities in the Glasgow area, brought about the first phased restoration plan for the canal, produced by the Scottish Inland Waterways Association in 1974. This plan, the underlying principles of which were largely incorporated into the official Canal Plan some years later, showed how each urban area could be linked to a reasonable length of open rural canal with a minimum number of obstructions being removed.

But the clean-up working parties and the country park plans and the restoration schemes being promoted by the voluntary groups had no official status, and events in 1974 proved that without some official policy for the canal, disaster could strike. Just as barge trips and small boat rallies were becoming popular in the area, Lanarkshire County Council decided to replace Glasgow Road Bridge, near Kirkintilloch, with an embankment and 3m. (10ft) diameter pipe sufficient only for small boats to pass through. Despite a strong campaign, Parliamentary questions, and even a private legal action, the pipe was installed. Just ten years later the Ferry Queen and Caledonian were based at the 'Stables' beside Glasgow Road Bridge but unable to pass through to Kirkintilloch. A costly new slipway had to be built for inspections and maintenance, with a £50,000 contribution from the new Regional Council. Six years later the culvert was replaced at considerable cost, the clearest possible example of how the apparently cheapest solution can eventually turn out to be the most expensive.

Following the loss of Glasgow Road Bridge, we decided to demonstrate that the canal was capable of being restored by clearing out lock chambers at Maryhill starting in 1975. By the following year, with sponsorship from Radio Clyde, both the top lock No 21, and No 23 were completely cleared of tons of silt and rubbish. To celebrate we held a tea party in the bottom of the top lock complete with white tablecloth and the Radio Clyde Canteen lady — who was ceremoniously lowered into the lock by crane.

Boats as a Campaigning Tool

Whilst lock chamber clearances were spectacular, it was clear that the Forth & Clyde Canal was too big to be restored by the same type of voluntary work that had been so successful on the English and Welsh narrow canals. Another problem was that few people in Central Scotland were aware of the concept of canals for cruising. Introducing such a concept could only be achieved by getting the public afloat.

Canal rallies and events were used to give people a taste of cruising. The first rally was at Ruchill Street, Maryhill, in August 1973 and repeated in 1974. The following year SIWA and the New Glasgow Society joined forces to organise a two-day rally at Bishopbriggs Sports Centre and Maryhill top lock. With the Strathkelvin Canal Park Group events in the Kilsyth/Cumberland area and SIWA and New Glasgow Society rallies at Bishopbriggs and Maryhill, all of a sudden there were boats on the water and people in the boats along much of the 25.7km. (16 miles) summit pound. It became obvious that getting people afloat on the canal had a far greater effect than any other form of propaganda.

The rallies, barge trips and galas of the seventies would not have been possible but for a great deal of work to enable the canal to be used, especially because of the greatly reduced water level. The early, purely cosmetic, clean-ups gave way to practical attempts to solve the main problems of getting boats in and out of the water and passengers in and out of the boats. The Strathkelvin Canal Park Group's working parties were engaged almost entirely on the construction of slipways and landing stages. At Wyndford Lock their landing stages were specifically designed for use by rowing eights during the annual Edinburgh University Regatta.

SIWA volunteers rebuilt sections of the collapsed canal bank at Temple and at Kirkintilloch to make it easier to use small boats and cleared many miles of the edge of the towpath to allow boats to be towed through heavy weed to reach rally sites. Volunteers also built the slipway at Sandbank Street in Maryhill and a large wooden landing stage, since demolished, outside the sports centre at Bishopbriggs. Much of the work by volunteers was continued by local authorities, making good use of the various job creation schemes in the late seventies and early eighties to resurface the towpath.

Radio Clyde's sponsorship in 1976 also led to a 3-day rally over the May holiday weekend with a day each in Kirkintilloch, Bishopbriggs and Maryhill. The impact of Clyde 76 was enormous. Apart from the constant publicity, the focus of the sponsorship was both on community involvement in improving the canal, and in enjoying it afterwards. A bandwagon effect had started: community councils started to take a lead in organising canalside events, and local authorities started to take notice.

Planning the Future

Whether it was the outcry over Glasgow Road Bridge or the canal's new found popularity, we never really knew what triggered the agreement in 1977 of all the local authorities to form a Technical Working Party of officials who, in 1979, recommended that a formal local plan be drawn up to guide and control developments on and around the canal for a 10-year period.

This interest by Local Authorities prompted SIWA members in the West to focus locally, and in April 1980 the Forth & Clyde Canal Society was formed. The new society grew rapidly, with particular early strength drawn from having many canalside community councils and similar groups as corporate members. Much of the society's early work was in conjunction with local bodies, continuing the earlier work of running boating events and barge trips for Gala Days and organizing joint clean-up working parties. A local canal society was also formed in Falkirk in 1980 to encourage local interest in both the Union and the Forth & Clyde canals, with considerable encouragement from Falkirk District Council.

The first draft plan, published by the authorities in October 1981, provided for a minimum height of new bridges and a phased scheme for re-opening substantial sections, similar to the scheme proposed by SIWA in 1974. The Canal Society made strenuous efforts to get people to comment on this and over 150 replies to the consultative draft were received by Strathclyde Regional Council, more than for the Structure Plan for the whole region. We were very determined: a Planner in the Council was given a copy of the Society membership list and he ticked off each member's reply as it arrived. Committee members then phoned any member who had not replied, so that by the end 70 per cent of the Society membership had put pen to paper! The policy that caused most comment was that on whether or not the canal should be refilled with water to its original level. Canal users pressed the extreme importance of restoring the water level to a height nearer to the top of the bank, which would provide an important contribution to safety and a more pleasing view. Getting this policy right was also crucial for the long term prospects for restoration because bridge heights would be determined by the water level.

A new draft of the plan produced in April 1984 caused dissent amongst the Canal Society, British Waterways and many of the District Councils by deleting the phased restoration programme and suggesting that restoration would be carried out 'as and when opportunities permitted', using the 'normal' resources available. The British Waterways Board's response was to suggest that an economic development study be prepared as a means of opening discussions with other funding agencies. A view began to emerge within the Canal Society that slow progress had some advantage because the process of debate generated by the plan's preparation was having a remarkable effect. As the years went by so the ambitions of both the enthusiasts and the authorities grew: indeed it seemed that the longer we waited for the plan to be completed, the more positive would be its outlook. Looking back on it, had we been saddled with a policy plan agreed in 1983–4, the whole future of the canal would have set out on a much less favourable course.

The Final Plan

The final version of the canal plan was opened up for public consultation between April and June 1987. Formal objections which had not been resolved were put to the test at a local public enquiry held in the Falkirk District Council chambers on 17 November 1987, presided over by a Scottish Office enquiry reporter.

The main difference of opinion between the canal society and the planning authorities lay in defining the navigational standards to be applied to the re-opened

Ferry Queen *and* Caledonian *at Bishopbriggs, 1990.*

Launch of Yarrow Seagull, *1984.*

canal. Whilst agreement had eventually been won on the height and width and depth of new bridges, it had been found that there was no definition of the length of craft that might pass through. The Society representatives, aided by an expert from the Inland Waterways Association and the owner of the restaurant boats based at the Ratho on the Union Canal, demonstrated successfully to the reporter how even new bridges, if poorly aligned, can be difficult for full length craft to negotiate. The enquiry found that such matters should not be left to chance and recommended that the local authorities adopt a planning policy that would ensure clear passage up to the same length as the locks.

The enthusiasts had also won major concessions. The long-standing argument over restoring the water to its original level was settled with a policy statement that consideration would be given to raising the water levels throughout the canal. As a consequence the plan was also amended to ensure that the possibility of the level being raised would be borne in mind by developers when planning the heights of new bridges. The local authorities also agreed to bring representatives of both the Forth & Clyde Canal Society and the Falkirk & District Canals Society onto a joint advisory committee to monitor the progress of the plan. In 1988, the plan was formally adopted as a policy to be used by all seven local authorities in decided planning applications which affected the canal, including potential new obstructions and the standards to be applied to new bridges.

Return of the Big Boats

The first restoration plans assumed that any progressive restoration would depend on the level of use that was being generated. Whilst the expected level of use by private boats never materialized, a more significant use by corporate and public trip boats emerged. By 1990 there were eight public trip boats operating on the canal. But how did this growth begin?

SIWA, and subsequently the Forth & Clyde Canal Society had dreamed of a return to the days of the famous 'Queens' but lacked the means to demonstrate this sort of cruising. In 1980 the Clyde Port Authority announced that their three remaining cross-harbour passenger ferries were coming out of service. Newspaper headlines enthused at the decision by the Forth & Clyde Society to buy the boats (on the strength of some generous loans by members). These boats were of a scale to match the canal and could carry 132 passengers. More importantly these 'Govan Ferries' carried with them the same kind of nostalgia reserved normally for trams: 'Dream of a cruise on the Govan Ferry' said the *Glasgow Herald*, whilst 'Clyde Ferries sail to life of leisure' was how the *Scotsman* announced the movement of the boats from Yorkhill on the Clyde to Bowling in May 1981, and in the wake of the ferries came a tide of goodwill for the Society and for the canal.

After a year of trial public trips using No 2 ferry between Bowling and Ferrydyke Bascule Bridge, an endless series of introductions, meetings, negotiations and letters produced grants totalling £5,000 to pay to move Ferry No 8 overland up to the summit reach. 'Speed Bonnie Boat up the Maryhill Road' reported the *Glasgow Herald* as astonished Glaswegians watched the 60-ton boat cruise through their streets on 14 April 1982. The boat made it safely to Hungryside Bridge, where author Lavinia Derwent launched her into the canal with the help of a bottle of champagne and a 250-ton mobile crane. Arranging the transport and launch required so much planning that the committee had not got around to discussing the name for the boat. A hastily convened pub lunch in the Stables produced a handwritten sign to be sellotaped to the hull minutes before she was launched, proclaiming her the *Ferry Queen*.

The *Ferry Queen* was soon joined at the Stables by the *Caledonian*, formerly Clyde Harbour Ferry No 10, converted into a restaurant boat for Caledonian Estates at the Rosneath Yard of D M Russell. This boat was fitted out with a full-length cabin and restaurant seating for 32 passengers. It was launched into the canal in November 1982, starting sailings before the year was out. 1984 saw the arrival of the first newly-built vessel on the canal. The *Yarrow Seagull* was built by the apprentice training school of British Shipbuilders at Yarrows on the Clyde for the Seagull Trust, a charity that provides free canal cruising for disabled people. To overcome the real possibility of vandalism the Trust had to build a boathouse and dry dock in Kirkintilloch at a cost of £80,000. The following year the *Govan Seagull* (built at the old Fairfields yard at Govan) was launched at Lock 16 in Falkirk for a temporary period before being moved up to the Union Canal, where full water levels and lower banks allowed a better view for passengers. *Lady Margaret,* a cruising restaurant boat, was launched in February 1987. She was designed to be low enough to pass under the Armco tube which was still at Glasgow Road Bridge, although the quantity of floating and submerged junk in the Kirkintilloch area at that time meant that the boat had to operate between the Stables and Bishopbriggs.

By this stage the Canal Plan had been adopted, including a policy which gave encouragement to the establishment of public trip boats. This eased the way for assistance from Local Authorities. In 1990 the *Gipsy Princess* was built at a cost of £25,000, raised by a generous grant from Cumbernauld & Kilsyth Council plus many fund raising events, and launched by the Forth & Clyde Canal Society to develop a service at Auchinstarry near Kilsyth, following three successful seasons using smaller boats.

In Glasgow a community project in Possilpark started a sailing club on Firhill Basin and later launched a large custom-built vessel, the *Nolly Barge,* to give residential cruises to local community and youth groups.

By the end of the eighties large passenger boats were carrying over 15,000 passengers a year. Smaller boats also started to return; occasional private boats were being trailed to the canal and voluntary society trip boats like *Auntie Kate* operated from the Union Inn by the Falkirk & District Canals Society, and *Alex Inglis* operated by the Forth & Clyde Canal Society. Cruising on the Forth & Clyde Canal was clearly not an elitist activity; it was for communities, charities and commerce – a powerful combination that in the latter days of the campaign ensured political support when it was needed most.

The Glasgow Canal Project

In 1988 British Waterways took everyone by storm in announcing an ambitious project to restore the 12 miles length from Temple to Port Dundas (on the Glasgow Branch) and to Kirkintilloch on the main line. The whole style of restoring the canal suddenly changed. The driving force behind the project was that a restored and used canal would increase the value of canalside land as demand for houses, pubs and leisure facilities beside the water increased. Re-opening the canal was to be on a commercial basis. Leisure was business and business was booming! 'The cash floodgates have opened,' reported the Glasgow *Evening Times* on the announcement.

The timing of the Glasgow Canal Project threw the phased restoration plan into touch. But the race to restore the canal in time, initially for the Glasgow Garden Festival in 1988, caused a strained relationship when cost cutting exercises suggested that bridges would be built below the standards still being discussed in the Canal Plan. Again, the Canal Society were drawn into a public debate, this time over the planning application for the reconstruction of Glasgow Road Bridge. An impassioned debate before the Planning Committee of Strathkelvin District Council in May 1988 resulted in a tied vote, the Chairman (the late Councillor Iain Nicolson) gave his casting vote to support the Canal Society's objection, so that planning permission would only be given for a bridge in keeping with the, as then only draft, proposals of the Canal Plan.

With the policy for bridge heights now tested successfully the Canal Society were able to give their full backing to the project and decided that as a show of complete support, *Ferry Queen's* operating base for 1988 should be in Glasgow. To get there, past the still un-reconstructed low bridge at Bishopbriggs, the superstructure had to be removed and replaced once she was past the bridge.

1988 also saw the opening of a reconstruction of Rockvilla Bridge at Applecross Street in Glasgow. The original wooden bascule bridge of that name was replaced with an electrically powered replica named after one of the canal builders, Robert Whitworth. The first bridge to be rebuilt was Firhill, closely followed by Glasgow Road Bridge, both re-opening in 1990, when to add to the bicentenary celebrations the top two locks at Maryhill were fully restored. Ruchill Street Bridge opened to canal traffic at the beginning of 1991. But still the primary aim of the project was frustrated by the low bridge at Bishopbriggs, a problem that remained with us until the final restoration.

Farm Bridge at Bishopbriggs, where the Glasgow Canal Project's hopes of restoring navigation between Glasgow and Kirkintilloch foundered in the early 1990s.

200th Anniversary – 1990: Year of the Rallies

1990 was a real challenge to both British Waterways and the various voluntary groups, being the 200th anniversary of the opening of the canal.

The biggest event of the bicentenary celebrations was held in Falkirk, in May, when the Inland Waterways Association National Trailboat Rally was held for the first time in Scotland. This was a three-day event held on new parkland reclaimed after the disastrous fire at Scottish Tar Distillers at Tamfourhill 17 years earlier. It was the biggest and most ambitious event ever held on the canal, with a small village being built beside the canal to accommodate the scores of volunteers from all parts of the UK. Every canal society contributed to the fleet of 9 trip boats available to give trips and to ferry visitors along or across the canal to reach the site.

Meanwhile in Glasgow, the Canal Society, British Waterways and a local organisation, Community Central Hall, formed a company to manage a full programme of canal events. *Ferry Queen* was chartered to the new joint group, with the trading name 'The Nolly Company' and was run with grants from local authorities and British Waterways five days a week by full time staff, who also organised pond dipping, small boat trips round Firhill Basin and historical walks around Port Dundas for schools. Later in the year the Nolly Company borrowed the replica *Vulcan* from the Summerlee Heritage Centre at Coatbridge and it became a floating exhibition centre at Applecross Street. By the end of the year, over 7,000 people had visited the canal in Glasgow on *Ferry Queen,* which was able to make use of the freshly restored top 2 locks at Maryhill. To enable *Ferry Queen* to operate reliably, British Waterways brought a floating dredger, a tug and two hoppers into action. *Ferry Queen* full of

Paddle power at Bishopbriggs during the Hogshead Rally, May 1990.

passengers passing the tug/barge unit full to the gunwales with mud was a sight that many had longed for.

In a variation on the canal marathon event, the Royal Naval Auxiliary Service and the Canal Society organised the 'Hogshead Rally', a fund-raising event which aimed to return to the River Forth the hogshead of water that was taken in 1790 to be poured into the River Clyde, but this time in a fleet of small boats each with a gallon container of water. All these years later it is safe to admit that the water they carried actually came from the tap at Bowling Basin, so that the re-levelling of Scotland's seas might be left to a more important occasion!

The canal's 200th anniversary year ended with a massive two-day birthday party at Maryhill locks, with some 20,000 visitors, bands playing, side-shows, stalls and, most unforgettably, both restored locks in constant use by boats. That event demonstrated a basic flaw in the idea that the local plan's limited restoration proposals would bring the canal back to life in urban areas. Most of the locks on this canal are in Glasgow and Falkirk, and for these areas to become busy and attractive they would have to become part of a through route as, apart from special events, little use would be made of locks that lead nowhere. The debate on whether the canal would ever be reopened from sea to sea was still in its infancy. Whilst the formal adoption of the Forth & Clyde Canal Local Plan was preventing any further infilling or low bridges, it was as though the idea of re-opening from sea to sea was the ambition that dare not speak its name for fear of ridicule at the cost.

Donald Mackinnon, who was chairman of the Forth & Clyde Canal Society in the early 1980s and took over as secretary in 1993, continues the story:

Threats and Promises

Ironically, after the Year of Rallies and the completion of the Glasgow Canal Project, the 1990s opened with a major, and potentially devastating, threat to the Canal. The proposed upgrading of the A80 to Motorway status was going to be a battle throughout the decade. The two options proposed were an upgrading of the existing road, called the Red Route, and a new road through the Kelvin Valley, called the Green Route. Whether it was deliberate cynicism or unintended irony, this so-called Green Route was anything but 'green'. It would have a catastrophic effect on the whole canal corridor, with no redeeming features. It would not remove the Castlecary blockage nor lead to any improvement of other canal crossings. As planned, this route would blight the entire area and jeopardise all that we had worked for. Unfortunately, this was the option favoured by the Scottish Development Department. The Society, supported by many other bodies, objected most strongly and resolved to fight this short sighted decision.

In January 1993 we gained the first concession when Lord James Douglas-Hamilton gave assurances that the removal of the Castlecary blockage would be considered an integral part of the A80/M80 upgrading, whichever route was chosen. Then in March 1997, after public consultation and a major campaign by the Society and many local groups, the Scottish Office reversed their preference on environmental grounds, and opted to upgrade the existing road to motorway standard. Two months later a Labour Government came to power, put the scheme on hold, and the newly created Scottish Executive shelved it in 1999 and later declared that the Kelvin Valley

Lock chamber clearance by volunteers at Temple, 1993.

would no longer be an option for upgrading the road. The battle had been won, although constant vigilance will be needed to combat any resurgence of the idea.

There were two promising developments at the beginning of the decade. 1991 saw the start of the Forth & Clyde Canal Community Project and the launch of the *Nolly Barge*. Both of these innovations were based in Maryhill in Glasgow and both would have a powerful role to play in the future. The following year, 1992, saw the removal of electricity cables under the Canal at Baird's Brae, right outside British Waterways offices. This led to a celebratory cruise into Spiers Wharf on 3 January 1993 by the largest gathering of boats seen since the heyday of Port Dundas.

However, 1993 was also a year in which we went back to our roots with a lock chamber clearance. To enable British Waterways to concentrate their limited resources on the installation of new lock gates, and thus do two locks instead of one, the Society took on the labour intensive task of clearing the accumulated muck and debris from the chambers of Locks 26 and 27. On 12 and 13 June, Society members, augmented by a team from Waterway Recovery Group and other canal societies, plunged into the mud of the partially drained pound. This was an ideal example of partnership in action.

Campaign for the 'Millennium Link'

Partnership was going to be the major theme of the years ahead. On 4 October 1994, British Waterways launched the bid for the 'Millennium Link', an ambitious and imaginative project, costing £78 million, to restore to navigation both the Union and

Forth & Clyde Canals. Despite the major benefits, both economically and environmentally, the initial bid was relegated to the 'B' list in June 1995. It transpired that the Millennium Commissioners were not convinced that the scheme had the support of the general public. The voluntary sector, led by the Forth & Clyde Canal Society, was determined to demonstrate that public support did indeed exist, and to this end launched a Declaration of Support. With a very limited time-scale, signing sessions were held along the entire canal corridor, resulting in almost 32,000 signatures being collected in six weeks.

On 30 November 1995, significantly St Andrew's Day, with pipes playing and Saltires flying, a delegation representing the full spectrum of canal users and enthusiasts presented the petition along with a revised bid to the Millennium Commission. This resulted in the scrapping of the 'A' and 'B' lists, and, on 26 April 1996, the 'Millennium Link' was back in contention. The campaign was given further impetus in May when the Society, playing away from home, took a leading role in a major Canal Festival at Wester Hailes in Edinburgh, a crucial battleground.

Though a lot of work was going on in the background, it was not until 14 February of the following year that the Millennium Commission announced their support with the award of £32 million. Unfortunately the long delays had meant that other schemes, though much later conceived, were now in direct competition. This was of particular significance in respect of European funding; the project had missed out on the current funding programme and had to compete for funds from the forthcoming tranche. As the year progressed, it became clear that the situation regarding the distribution of European funding was becoming extremely serious for the scheme. This precipitated

Lock chamber clearance, Millennium Link style:
a digger removes infill from Lock 32, Blairdardie.

Rolling out the liner for the new section of canal leading to the sea-lock on the River Carron.

Creating the channel beside the fish and chip ship at Clydebank.

a round of frantic activity and in December all the partners, including the voluntary sector, resolved on a course of vigorous action. This was a major turning point in the campaign, as on 6 April 1998 the Scottish Office announced their approval of the necessary European funding. The total package of £78.4 million was now complete. The funding partners consisted of the Millennium Commission with the largest contribution of over £32 million, the rest of the money coming from the seven Local Authorities, British Waterways, the Scottish Enterprise Network, and the European Regional Development Fund. The voluntary sector's contribution of £1.6 million was calculated in kind rather than in cash.

The agreement between all the funding partners and British Waterways was formally signed in Glasgow City Chambers on 12 February 1999, and the 'Millennium Link' was officially declared underway at a ceremony on 12 March, when the late Donald Dewar cut the first sod at Blairdardie, on the Forth & Clyde Canal. Once again, the Society played a prominent role as our flagship, the *Gipsy Princess*, conveyed the dignitaries to the site.

Building 'The Link'

While the project would eventually restore 108km. (67 miles) of canal including the 51km. (31.7 miles) of the Union Canal, the task of restoration of the Forth & Clyde was daunting enough on its own. This would entail the construction of 17 new fixed bridges, the refurbishment of 2 opening bridges and construction of 2 new opening road bridges, plus 2 new opening pedestrian bridges. At several locations the construction of the new bridge was the easy part, the diversion of services being

Partially filled, narrowed channel
between the new and old Lock 5 at Bainsford, Falkirk.

Provost McSkimming re-opened Kirkintilloch's Townhead Bridge on 21 May 2000 . . .

. . . and two hours later Adam Lawton re-opened Farm Bridge at Bishopbriggs with a giant pair of scissors.

frequently a greater and more expensive problem. It is not often realised what a mass of pipes and cables, carrying everything from gas to fibre optics, were buried within bridge structures. As well as the new sea-lock to the River Carron, four new locks had to be built and all the others refurbished and, in many cases, regated. As well as standard locks, a unique drop-lock had also to be built. To complete the task facing the engineers, a total of 1.4km. (1,530yds) of new canal channel had to be dug.

This simple list conceals some really superb feats of civil engineering to overcome major obstacles. One such was constructing the Canal under the A80, where disruption to traffic was kept to the minimum by re-routing traffic so that one carriageway was kept open at all times. Another complex contract was in Glasgow where the Canal had been infilled for 400m. (440yds) and Great Western Road culverted. The solution was to dig a new channel, excavate and rebuild a lock-chamber, build an entirely new road, and construct a footbridge as well as the dual carriageway road bridge. The low level crossing of the Canal at Dalmuir, combined with adjacent road junctions and the proximity of housing, meant that raising the road was not possible. The only alternative was to lower the Canal. A drop-lock had to be constructed which would allow vessels to be lowered to a level where they could sail under the road before the re-filled lock would once again raise them to the normal level.

A massive programme of dredging, weed cutting and rubbish removal had also to be carried out to give the minimum depth required for the initial re-opening. This programme will continue, progressively increasing the depth to accommodate deeper draught sea-going yachts.

As so much of the Society's efforts had been in the Kirkintilloch area, it was fitting that the first re-opened section of Canal to be celebrated was from Kirkintilloch to Bishopbriggs. On 21 May 2000 a fleet of vessels of all shapes and sizes sailed through the new Townhead Bridge replacing the drowned culvert that had effectively cut the summit in half. Equally fitting for a town famed for building puffers, a pair of enthusiasts had built a replica, the *Wee Spark*, which took its place in the convoy through Kirkintilloch. From there the flotilla sailed under the raised bridge at Cadder and the new Farm Bridge on Balmuildy Road in Bishopbriggs. It was also significant that while Townhead Bridge was officially opened by the Society President, the Provost and the Member of Parliament, it was a young boy representing the next generation who opened Farm Bridge. The future is in its hands.

Despite the magnitude of the task of restoration, the target for re-opening the Forth & Clyde Canal to navigation by May 2001 was met. British Waterways had excelled themselves once again. On 26 May 2001 the Society vessels, *Gipsy Princess* and *Janet Telford*, were prominent among the boats gathered at Lock 16 in Falkirk to welcome the first of the yachts coming up the long climb from the River Forth. From there the fleet sailed on an epic journey to Bowling, reaching the River Clyde on 28 May. This was a truly historic occasion: the day we had dreamt of, and fought for, for over thirty years, had at last dawned. The Forth & Clyde Canal was once again open to through navigation. The Society flagship, the *Gipsy Princess*, was again to the fore on 12 June in Grangemouth when HRH Prince Charles performed the ceremonial pouring of a hogshead of water from the River Clyde into the River Forth – the reverse of the ceremony at the canal's opening in 1790 when a barrel of water from the Forth was poured into the Clyde to symbolise the union of the eastern and western seas.

The next step will be when the Forth & Clyde Canal is once again linked to the Union Canal, thus restoring navigation between Glasgow and Edinburgh. No longer by a long flight of locks, but by an innovative design typifying twenty-first century engineering, the great Falkirk Wheel. This unique construction, a rotating boat lift, will stand 35m. (115ft) high and be 28m. (92ft) in length. The massive structure, weighing 1,800 tons complete with 500,000 litres (110,000 gallons) of water, will be capable of lifting several small boats or a large vessel up to 21m. (70ft) in length. The cycle will take 15 minutes to transfer boats from one canal to the other. The visual impact of the Wheel, combined with the graceful aqueduct springing from the hillside, will ensure that this will take its place as one of Scotland's greatest tourist attractions.

It is important to keep in mind that while our campaign for restoration of navigation may be over, this is only a new beginning for the Forth & Clyde Canal. It is also a new beginning for the Forth & Clyde Canal Society which will have to redirect its energies to ensure that the project succeeds in delivering the regenerative benefits to canalside communities we always said it would. More campaigning, more work and more dedication will be needed if what the Millennium Link has started is to be converted into a new and perhaps greater canal age.

'Millie' the giant fish that led the parade to reopen the canal in May 2001.

Wildlife   Olivia Lassière

In the two centuries since the Forth & Clyde Canal was carved through the farmed and wooded landscape of the central belt of Scotland, this man-made habitat has attracted wildlife throughout its length. Some of the plants and animals have found their way naturally into the waterway and others have been 'helped in' by man's activities. In this chapter, I hope to introduce you to some of the plant and animal characters that you might come across during visits to the canal and its associated habitats. Whatever the season or time of day, city or countryside, you will be sure to see life along the canal. This chapter aims to give you a flavour of the potential wildlife safari on your doorstep and to provide tips for things to look out for on your next trip.

Looking for Wildlife

No specialist equipment is required to see wildlife on the canal but a pair of binoculars, a hand lens, a pond net and a tray will ensure that the microscopic and the distant get a closer look. If you are keen to name what you see there are many excellent wildlife guidebooks on the market or available in your local library. Whatever you do, please remember to dress for the weather and take care when near the water and lock chambers.

No Place like Home: the Habitats of Plants and Animals on the Canal

British Waterways' land holdings for the Forth & Clyde Canal and its feeders extend to approximately 410ha, with the canal open water area covering approximately 110ha. This is a relatively small water body when compared with one of Scotland's largest lochs, Loch Lomond, which covers an area of 7,636ha. The Forth & Clyde Canal at 56km. (34.5 miles) long is, however, a significant wet corridor when compared with the Rivers Forth and Clyde which are approximately 64km. (39.7 miles) and 96km. (59.6 miles). long respectively. Within the boundary of this relatively small land area, the canal network provides a whole host of places for animals and plants to inhabit:

- canal channel and waterway banks,
- reedbeds
- grassed towpath verges
- hedgerows and other field margins
- scrub and woodland
- cuttings and embankments
- bridges, locks and buildings
- supply reservoirs and feeder streams
- adjoining land

The following sections take each habitat (home) in turn and give you a flavour of what you might expect to find there. In reality, many of these habitats merge with each other and animal species move between them, so the descriptions which follow are only indicative. The diagram shows a cross section through a typical canal channel showing habitats, so bear in mind that there are local variations.

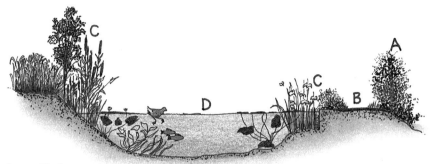

A: Hedgerow.
B: Towpath and grassed towpath verges.
C: Waterway banks with emergent fringe and retaining wall.
D: Canal channel.

The Wet Channel

As a waterway in Scotland, the Forth & Clyde Canal is unique because it crosses the catchments of two large rivers, the Forth and the Clyde, and animals and plants which might otherwise be geographically separated have come into contact with each other. This, coupled with nearly two centuries of natural colonisation, boat traffic and uncontrolled 'introductions', has contributed to a living 'melting pot' and a biologically unique waterway in Scottish terms.

The most obvious canal habitat is the wet channel itself, which is more akin to a long narrow loch than a river. It has also been compared to the slow-flowing stretch of a river or the margin of a productive loch. The canal channel does, however, have some properties which make it a unique wildlife habitat:

1.   In the days of frequent canal traffic, the puddle clay lining of the bottom was subject to slow but continuous scouring, producing a layer of silt. This was not deposited evenly on the bottom – greater accumulations occurred at the edges, often with the formation of lateral shelves. In contrast, the central portion of the canal was maintained as a uniformly deep channel. The variation in profile that this produced provided a variety of habitats for plants and animals.
2.   The lining itself acts as a seal, preventing changes that would otherwise be caused by local variations in geology.
3.   The water level is stable, so that the canal is not subject to the destructive scouring of rivers in flood, or the drying of the bed in a hot summer.
4.   The relative shallowness, originally up to 2.7m. (9ft) deep, allows sunlight to penetrate to the bottom in most areas and ensures thorough mixing of the water

throughout its depth. It is a common feature of lochs, by contrast, that nutrients are often trapped in deeper water under a warm surface layer.

5.   The canal receives an abundant supply of nutrients from its feeders and also in run-off, rich in fertilisers from agricultural land.
6.   The average flow of 22.7 million litres (5 million gallons) per day, while not strong enough to displace plant roots, continuously replaces nutrients such as phosphate and nitrate, supplies oxygen and removes waste products and pollution.
7.   The flow rate creates slow currents in wide areas and faster currents in narrow sections, further increasing the habitat diversity available to plants and animals.
8.   Apart from the summit pound, the water is being continuously aerated as it falls over lock gates and weirs.

Aquatic Plants

As a result of the conditions described above, the canal channel provides the ideal growing conditions for a whole range of truly aquatic plants. Vegetation surveys along the entire canal in 1988 and 1997 recorded an impressive 31 species of aquatic plants using every zone of water space, making the canal an extremely important water body for aquatic plant diversity in Scotland.

Floating on the surface, with their roots hanging free in the water, three small species of duckweed, the gibbous, common and ivy-leaved and Frogbit, which looks like a small water lily, may been seen. These plants are often at the mercy of water currents and surface winds; rafts of them are blown up and down the canal and are often caught behind obstructions, forming dense mats.

Rooted in the sediment with both submerged and floating leaves are starworts, broad leaved pondweed and yellow and white water lilies. The yellow water lilies, which occur along half the length of the canal, are easy to spot with their large oval leaves and prominent yellow flowers. They make a wonderful spectacle in June and July and are often frequented by mating damselflies. The canal is also home to a rare hybrid water lily, *Nuphar* x *spennerana* which occurs in the Dullatur Marsh Site of Special Scientific Interest, just east of Kilsyth.

Yellow water lily.

Willow moss favours the hard surfaces of bridges and waterway walls just below the water surface. The amphibious bistort only produces floating leaves and has a distinctive pink flower spike.

Other plants are true water specialists and remain completely submerged: e.g. stoneworts , Rigid hornwort, Canadian and Nuttall's pondweed, which are introduced plants, Spiked water milfoil, 11 species of pondweed (*Potamogeton alpinus, P.berchtoldii, the rare hybrid P.x.bennettii, P.crispus, P.friesii, P.lucens, P.obtusifolius, P.perfoliatus, P.pusillus, P.trichoides*), and horned pondweed. *Potamogeton* x *bennettii*, a hybrid of *P.crispus* and *P.trichoides*, is of particular interest because the canal and some adjacent streams are the only locations in Britain where it is known to occur. Unbranched bur-reed has long ribbon like leaves which form beds under water.

Aquatic Invertebrates

With this range of aquatic plants, and other potential habitats such as bottom sediment, solid surfaces of built structures, open water column and water surface, it is no surprise that the animal life is equally diverse in the wet channel. A quick swish of a pond net will soon reveal the sheer variety. Dominating the invertebrate scene are the snails and mussels (Mollusca), segmented worms (Oligochaeta) and hoglice or water slaters. Fifteen species of mollusc, including the lake limpet, wandering snail, greater ramshorn and the great pond snail have been recorded from the canal. These shelled creatures are a clear indication of the mineral rich waters of the canal. The water snails are vegetarian and feed on water plants or, more commonly, the film of algae which covers most submerged objects. By contrast, the pea mussels (*Pisidium* spp.) are filter feeders which burrow into the bottom sediments and are a staple food item of many fish and water birds.

Other sediment dwellers include voracious alder fly (*Sialis lutaria*) larvae and blood worms (Chironomidae), which are, in fact, the larvae of dancing midges that often form large swarms hovering above the water during the summer. Hoglice and segmented worms also spend their lives in or on the sediment. In amongst the weeds, you may find caddis fly larvae with protective cases made of vegetation, shells or stone particles, freshwater shrimps, biting midge larvae, beetles (both larval and adult forms), leeches, flatworms, damselfly and dragonfly larvae and the occasional mayfly, greater and lesser water boatmen and the curious water scorpion, whose long tail is actually a breathing tube. The most impressive beetle is the great diving beetle (*Dytiscus marginalis*), clearly recognisable with its livery of black rimmed with gold. Both the adult and larval forms are keen predators, enjoying a diet of small fish, tadpoles and other invertebrates. If you find one of these beasts take care, as they will also bite unwary collectors' fingers!

On the water surface specialist hunters like the long legged pond skaters and whirligig beetles can often be seen. The whirligig beetles are specially adapted for their life at the air-water interface with 'double function' eyes that can see prey above and below the water line.

A group of animals that deserve special mention are the freshwater sponges which take two forms in the canal, either yellow and encrusting or with a growth form similar to long green fingers. Look out for discarded bicycles, old branches and submerged structures which are often adorned with sponges.

In the open water, planktonic creatures, both plant and animal, abound, many of which are so small that a microscope is required to see them properly. The larger planktonic animals include the water fleas for which the Forth & Clyde is well known. A survey in the 1980s recorded 33 species, including *Alona weltneri*, which was only the second time this species had been found anywhere in the UK.

Fish

With the wealth of plant and invertebrate life, the canal has developed into an important coarse fishery which is recognised internationally under the auspices of the European Freshwater Fisheries Directive. The most commonly seen fish in the canal are the pike, perch, roach, tench and eels. Fish rescues as part of the Millennium Link project and records from fishermen have revealed some fine specimens including 900mm (3ft) pike, 490mm (1.6ft) tench and 1.7kg (3.75lb.) eels. Other species known to live in the canal include carp, bream, three-spined stickleback, minnow and ruffe. Some of the fish, like the silver bodied shoaling roach, feed on weed and small invertebrates, while others, like pike and perch, are carnivorous creatures and feed

Roach.

almost exclusively on invertebrates, other fish and the occasional duckling! The aquatic plants in the channel perform several functions which are important to fish; oxygen release, provision of egg laying sites and hiding places for young fry and even a direct food source or a habitat for invertebrate prey items like snails.

Other Vertebrates

The most obvious wildlife on the canal is the wildfowl. For many, feeding the ducks and swans is one of the great pleasures of a canal visit. On the water, you are most likely to see mute swans, mallard, coot and moorhen. Swans are particularly noticeable during the breeding season and often make huge nests out of vegetation and discarded household items. Eighteen pairs were confirmed as breeding in 1997 along the canal. Some pairs even make their nests on the towpath, so take care as you pass. The coots and moorhens are more shy and make their nests amongst the reedy fringe or on floating objects in the canal. Less common are little grebe, found in the western section of the Forth & Clyde, and tufted duck. Herons are often seen stalking for fish along the shallows of the canal. They are also partial to the occasional frog.

Frogs, toads and newts, both palmate and smooth, breed in the canal

Swan's nest with pram at Kirkintilloch.

Moorhen on nest.

and massive shoals of tadpoles can be seen in the shallows in early summer. When fully grown, these animals leave the water and forage amongst the bank side vegetation for invertebrates. A house owner in Bonnybridge has reported a regular invasion of small frogs coming into her canal-side home every summer!

Other cold-blooded animals in the canal include red-eared terrapins, which can be seen basking on warm days. These are obviously discarded pets which can live for up to 100 years. The cold Scottish climate should prevent them from breeding successfully.

Otters are known to frequent the canal and have been seen swimming across the canal at Kirkintilloch and signs of otter have been recorded at Cadder, Wyndford and Possil. These animals are most active at night, so you may catch a glimpse of one on an evening walk. Late night trips may also reward you with the sight of bats, both pipistrelle and Daubenton's, as they fly over the water surface searching for an insect meal. In daylight hours, swallows, swifts and sand martins also take advantage of this aerial insect larder.

Waterway Banks

Waterway banks at the edge of the canal, where land and water meet, provide us with some of the greatest diversity of plant and animal life on the canal. In this transition zone, the fringing vegetation is dominated by emergent plants whose roots are permanently below the water line and plants which prefer to root themselves in damp ground above the water line.

Twenty-one species of emergent plants have been recorded along the canal. Reed sweet-grass (*Glyceria maxima*) with its characteristic glossy, green leaves with boat shaped tips, is the most common, occurring throughout the entire length of the canal channel from Grangemouth to Bowling. This canal abundance belies its rarity outside the Lowland Canal network in Scotland. Iris,

Reed sweet grass.

Tufted loosestrife. *Arrowhead.*

with its distinctive 'fleur-de-lis' yellow flower, flote grass, reed canary grass, water cress, reed mace and the introduced arrowhead make up the rest of the regular elements of this emergent fringe. The nationally scarce tufted loosestrife, easily recognised by its paired leaves and stalked yellow flowers, is also common at the waters edge. Some of these plants were probably introduced by the early canal companies as a form of green engineering to combat erosion!

Less frequently seen are brooklime with delicate blue flowers, common reed which grows to 3.5m. (12ft), sweet-flag, which has a fragrance of tangerines, and branched bur-reed, with characteristic branches of spherical seed heads. The narrow-leaved water plantain (*Alisma lanceolatum*) is extremely rare in Scotland and has its stronghold in the canal. It is recognised by its spear shaped leaves arising from below the water surface and is said to only open its flowers between 9am and 2pm unlike the more common water plantain between 1 and 7pm!

The emergent plants provide cover and nesting areas for water birds, food for water voles, a home and hunting ground for amphibians and stems for aquatic insects to emerge and overwinter. Water vole numbers have declined significantly over the last 20 years across the UK. The canal provides suitable food plants for voles but predation pressure from mink appears to keep the numbers down. There are a few records for water voles around Wyndford, at the Falkirk Wheel site and Auchinstarry. A comprehensive survey of these animals this summer (2001) will establish their current status. Sadly, the number of sightings of mink is increasing which means the future of the water vole population is not bright.

Further up the bank, species tolerant of damp ground abound and merge with the towpath grasslands. These include the frequently occurring white frothy flowered meadow sweet, creeping buttercup, angelica, great willowherb, gipsywort bittersweet, valerian and greater bird's-foot-trefoil.

Reedbeds

True reed beds consisting of extensive stands of common reed (*Phragmites australis*) are uncommon on the Forth & Clyde. Small stands are present at Dullatur Marsh and at the eastern end of the canal leading to the River Carron. These support a range of birds, notably reed bunting and a variety of invertebrates.

Water vole.

Valerian.

Grassed Towpath Verges

Grasslands seen along the towpath only exist as a result of management which prevents the invasion of scrub vegetation. On the canal, there are few grazers (rabbits and deer) so it is the twice yearly cut (spring and autumn) by British Waterways which maintains this habitat on the waterway. This regime was devised to maximise wildlife benefit of the grassland while allowing our human customers relatively easy passage along the towpath. By cutting late on in the year, the grass and herb species are able to flower and set seed. Not only does this provide a food source for insects, birds and small mammals but also it ensures a healthy sward in following years.

In summer, this grassland is full of a wonderful array of plants, many of which were used by people for herbal remedies in the days before the National Health Service. Of these, you will find the pink flowered valerian, known for its stress-relieving properties, sweet cicely, a cure for flatulence, and meadowsweet which was used as an air freshener and cold remedy and was the plant from which the active ingredient for aspirin was first isolated in the early nineteenth century.

Close to the waterway, towpath verges support many meadow plants such as the valerian and meadowsweet described above. Other characteristic wet meadow plants, like the marsh bedstraw, also occur. Two orchid species are also found in this habitat; Common spotted orchid and the much rarer Northern marsh orchid are worth looking out for.

On the hedgerow side of the towpath, there are dry meadow plants such as cow parsley, red campion, oxeye daisy, black knapweed and two species of thistle. Fireweed and broad-leaved willow-herb which occur throughout the canal length provide a bright splash of colour. Grasses are common here with the taller Yorkshire Fog, False oat grass and

Meadowsweet in flower.

Tufted vetch.

Cock's foot being most obvious. Members of the pea family, Meadow vetchling and tufted vetch, climb amongst the towpath plants.

On the path itself only the more trample resistant plants such as ribwort and greater plantain, and dandelions survive.

Invertebrates take advantage of the towpath verges too. Beetles, hover-flies, millipedes, centipedes, woodlice and snails can all be found. Bumblebees are often particularly common, feeding on towpath flowers and nesting in the soil.

The mat of dead vegetation along the towpath that accumulates in the course of time may harbour numerous small mammals, which can often be heard if not seen. These small mammals are food for a number of larger predators. The kestrel is a common sight at any season right into urban areas. Roe deer, fox and badger will all use the towpath. If you are lucky you may also get a glimpse of a stoat or weasel as it crosses

85

the path. Evidence for these is most likely to be indirect as droppings, fur, remains of kills and prints. If you doubt the scale of the animal traffic along your local section of canal towpath, walk it after a snowfall.

Hedgerows and Other Field Margins

Hawthorn.

Hedgerows were established when the canal was built to define the boundary of the canal company land. Today, along with canal-side trees, they form an important landscape feature and offer nesting sites and perching posts for birds including grasshopper warbler, whitethoat, grey partridge, yellow hammer, linnet, bullfinch, blackbird, robin and chaffinch. Hedgehogs, bank voles, shrews and wood mice all use the canal hedgerow habitats for shelter and food. Moles sometimes leave tell tale piles of soil where they have been along the towpath. Hedgerows also provide food, in the form of leaves, flowers, fruits, seeds and sap for a wide range of animals, particularly insects. An early summer treat is the sight of the orange tipped butterfly, whose larvae thrive on hedgerow species like garlic mustard and lady's smock.

Most of the tree and shrub species found along the towpath are native to Britain. The list includes willows of various types, the common and stock proof hawthorn, blackthorn, elder, alder, oak, ash, birch, wych elm, crab apple, bird cherry and dog rose. Some hedgerow species, like raspberry and bramble also provide a tasty morsel for towpath walkers. Snowberry occurs occasionally along the canal and it was introduced to the UK as cover for game birds.

As with grasslands, much of the wildlife value of hedgerows depends on active management.

Scrub and Woodland

The undisturbed offside bank in some sections of the canal has developed into scrub and woodland. Ash and sycamore woodland, alder and downy birch woodland and willow woodland are all frequent along the Forth & Clyde Canal. With appropriate management these areas can support good numbers of woodland birds e.g. tree sparrow, blackcap and whinchat, woodland mammals and a varied woodland flora.

In some areas cut branches are left to form habitat piles for hibernating amphibians. Dead trees can also provide roosting sites for bats and perfect conditions for the establishment of fungi. Living and dead trees often support varied lichen floras.

Cuttings and Embankments

Cuttings and embankments create another dimension for wildlife establishment on the canal. Here steeply engineered slopes can provide woodland, grassland, scrub and open rock habitats. It is here that barn owls, which have declined as a result of intensive farm management, may find their small mammal prey which they hunt for at dusk.

The alien plant, Japanese knotweed, *Fallopia japonica*, is established at various points along the canal on embankments and in areas where hedgerow plants might otherwise flourish. Recent research suggests that these aliens do support some wildlife species. It will be important to monitor the spread of this plant to devise the most appropriate management strategy over the coming years.

Japanese knotweed.

Bridges, Locks and Buildings

Canal structures are perhaps less obvious wildlife habitats. On closer inspection you may be surprised by the wide range of mosses, liverworts and lichens, most of which have unpronounceable Latin names, that live on canal side walls, buildings and bridges. Budding bryologists and lichenologist would have a field day! Some of the lichens grow very slowly, so may be as old as the canal itself.

Ferns also favour old structures and many grow out of the old wooden piling along the canal edge or stone abutments of bridges. The royal fern, a firm favourite with Victorian fern collectors, grows on the walls at Port Dundas in

Wall rue.

Glasgow and at Balmuildy Bridge in Bishopbriggs. Wall rue prefers calcareous soils and grows successfully in structures where lime rich mortar has been used.

Take a look next time you pass through a lock chamber and you will be surprised by the small ferns, mosses, woodlice and millipedes which seem to thrive in these apparently hostile places. Birds too occasionally nest on canal structures. Grey wagtails have nested on pontoons and pigeons on lock gates in recent years. Foxes are regular evening visitors to the British Waterways office grounds at Glasgow.

Supply Reservoirs and Feeder Streams

The Forth and Clyde supply reservoirs and their feeder streams offer further additional wildlife habitats on the network. Hillend and Black Lochs, for example, are quite high up in the catchment and support flora and fauna typical of nutrient poor (oligotrophic) standing waters. Hillend Loch for example supports winter flocks of wildfowl including mallard, pochard and tufted duck. Black Loch Moss SSSI, adjacent to Black Loch, is an important area of raised mire (bog) vegetation. The feeder streams will support animals and plants which are adapted to high flow rates. Kingfishers have been reported from the summit pound feeder at Kilsyth.

The principal feeder for the western end of the Forth & Clyde canal is the Monkland Canal, much of which is piped under the M8. The open sections of canal are important for wildlife and have been designated as a wetland 'Site of Local Ecological Importance' by North Lanarkshire Council.

Adjoining Land

Areas of land next to the canal corridor, such as gardens, industrial estates and parks also benefit wildlife. The new extension of the Forth & Clyde to the River Carron adds another dimension to the canal wildlife interest. Here you will have a chance to see coastal species like cormorant, shelduck and common tern.

Recognition of Importance

This man-made waterway is recognised at local, national and international level as an important wildlife asset. Its linear route has allowed organisms more commonly associated with rural areas to enter the towns and industrialised areas bringing a green ribbon of life to the areas through which it passes. The principal point of access is the towpath, which means much of the opposite bank or offside is left undisturbed and is therefore an important haven for plants and animals alike. In the countryside changes in farming practice, particularly mechanisation and the widespread use of agro-chemicals, have led to the loss of much rural wildlife during the same period, so that the role of the canal as a haven for wildlife may extend beyond the boundaries of our urban conurbations.

The value placed on these wildlife habitats on the canal corridor is reflected in the number of statutory and non-statutory wildlife sites designated along the Forth & Clyde. Statutory sites include two wetland sites, Dullatur Marsh Site of Special Scientific Interest (SSSI) and Possil Marsh SSSI. Dullatur Marsh SSSI is the only on channel SSSI and is part of the Kelvin Valley Marshes wetland system. The site supports fen vegetation, marshy grassland, open water, wet woodland and breeding birds including water rail, teal, snipe, grasshopper warbler, whinchat and mute swan. In winter the site is important for jacksnipe and snipe and other wintering and passage waders and wildfowl.

Adjacent to new sea route leading to Lock 2 at Grangemouth is Skinflats SSSI. This site is a large intertidal bay on the inner Forth estuary with mudflat, saltmarsh and coastal lagoon habitats and is known for wintering wildfowl and wader populations, in particular shelduck. In winter over 100 different species regularly occur including dunlin, golden plover, pintail, bar-tailed godwit and peregrine.

The Inner Clyde Estuary Special Protection Area (SPA) abuts the Bowling Terminus of the canal. This site holds internationally important numbers of wintering redshank and nationally important numbers of wintering cormorant, scaup, eider, goldeneye, red breasted merganser, oystercatcher and curlew.

The Firth of Forth SPA, through which boaters pass as they approach the eastern terminus of the canal, is a vast area of intertidal flats and inshore water important for wintering wildfowl and waders. The site is internationally important for wintering pink-footed geese, knot, bar-tailed godwit, redshank and turnstone and nationally important for wintering great crested grebe, cormorant, seven species of wildfowl and two species of wader and for breeding common and little terns.

Ancient woodlands occur adjacent to the canal between Bonnybridge and Falkirk and at Roman Camp west of Falkirk.

There are numerous non-statutory wildlife sites, designated by the Scottish Wildlife Trust and local authorities, on or adjacent to the canal. Examples include Roughcastle in Falkirk with woodland, wet heath, acid grassland and semi-improved grassland habitats and Barhill Site of Importance for Nature Conservation (SINC) which supports woodland wet meadows and lies west of Auchinstarry. The Saltings SINC in Old Kilpatrick adjacent to the canal has a range of brackish swamp, scrub and grassland habitats. The latter supports meadow brown and common blue butterflies.

Dullatur Marsh SSSI.

Looking after our Natural Assets

The opening of the Forth & Clyde Canal heralds a new era with, among other things, exciting opportunities for environmental management, development and recreation. British Waterways is well aware of the importance of the canal's wildlife and through sensitive management will seek to enhance and maintain its value. Wildlife survey information collected prior to the Millennium Link works has set a baseline against which to monitor change. A monitoring programme will examine the impacts of increased boat traffic on the wildlife resource.

British Waterways, through partnership with local authorities and other environmental representatives, will seek to manage wildlife habitats sustainably through the development and implementation of local Biodiversity Action Plans (BAPs) and a Lowland Canal BAP by 2005. These plans will guide the sensitive management of our existing and newly created habitats such as the canal channel extension in Grangemouth. They also serve to highlight potential projects which will improve the linkage between the canal and other wildlife habitats e.g. woodland planting.

Taking a Look

So there is no time to lose, take the opportunity to make your own wildlife spotting excursions. Alternatively you could join our ranger on the canal or take part in volunteer recording of wildlife from birds to bats to water voles and water ferns. After all, a lot of what we know about wildlife on the canal, has come from the records of dedicated volunteers.

Parts of this chapter are based on the original wildlife text by David Lampard and Clive Morgan in the second edition of the Guidebook.

Enjoying the Canal Paul Carter

The newly restored canal offers many ways to get away from it all. With 55km. (34 miles) of cruising water and a further 52km. (32 miles) along the Union Canal, the inland cruiser can enjoy a wide variety of country and town landscapes, and can sail to both of Scotland's principal cities of Glasgow and Edinburgh. Passage can once again be made from the North Sea to the Atlantic Ocean. A round trip through the Forth and Clyde Canal, Crinan and Caledonian canals, takes in the finest inter-island cruising in Europe. Public trip boats and restaurant barges ply the canal and local canoe clubs are based on the canal banks. As well as getting afloat, there is plenty to enjoy along the towpath. Fishing, cycling and walking are all popular, with the canal's rich wildlife and history giving plenty to see, and pubs and restaurants for refreshment.

Private Cruising

British Waterways publish a free *Skipper's Guide* which is an absolute must for anyone wanting to cruise along the canal. The guide gives general information, maps, and details of safety, pilotage, lock operation and boat licenses. It can be obtained from their offices or on line at www.scottishcanals.co.uk.

From the Clyde end, boats enter the canal through the sea lock from Bowling Harbour into Bowling Basin. Nineteen locks lift the canal a total of 47.5m. (156ft) in a distance of 14.2km. (8.8 miles) from the Clyde to the summit reach at Maryhill. There is a drop lock at Dalmuir, created to allow passage beneath a major road. Ten of the locks are concentrated in two main flights, at Cloberhill and Maryhill.

From Maryhill the 3km. (2 miles) long Glasgow branch heads south-east into Glasgow and the 26km. (16 miles) summit pound heads east through Kirkintilloch to Wyndford. A further 19 locks drop the canal over a 15km. (9 miles) stretch through Falkirk to the River Carron at Grangemouth, including the new double height sea lock. Thirteen of these locks are concentrated in a 3km. (2 miles) stretch in Falkirk. The magnificent Falkirk Wheel is situated on the western outskirts of the town. Boats can use the Wheel to access the Union Canal and Edinburgh.

DIMENSIONS

Locks

Rise	2.4m.	8ft
Length	20.9m.	68.5ft
Width	6.0m.	19.7ft

Canal

Top Width	18.0m.	60ft
Depth around	1.8m.	6ft

*The 1998 Kilsyth Gala Queen and her entourage
on board* **Gipsy Princess** *at Auchinstarry.*

There are several lifting or swing bridges along the route together with many fixed bridges. The fixed bridges all have a minimum clearance of 3m. (10ft). The canal generally has a top width of around 18m. (60ft) but there are narrow stretches close to some bridges, and also substantially wider stretches between Auchinstarry and Wyndford The central channel is generally dredged to 1.8m. (6ft) depth but beware submerged obstructions such as shopping trolleys particularly near bridges and in urban areas. See Chapter 1 for a more detailed description of the route, Appendix 1 for more details of bridges and locks, and British Waterways for essential information including operating instructions.

Mooring alongside the towpath is not practicable along the whole length of the canal as canal water level is generally maintained at a level of around 0.5 to 0.9m. (1.5 to 3.0ft) below the original water level, and hence well below the coping level. The thick reed growth and shallow depth near the bank are further obstacles to mooring. Mooring is however possible at many locations such as close to locks, bridges, and old wharves, but care must be taken to avoid obstruction. Permanent moorings together with other facilities such as water supply, toilets etc. are available or planned at Bowling Basin, Auchinstarry Basin, and Carron Sea Lock. Slipways are available at Maryhill, Firhill and Applecross Street Basin in Glasgow, the Stables and South bank Road Kirkintilloch and Auchinstarry. See Appendix 2 for further details of moorings and slipways. Facilities are likely to be added to at any time, see British Waterways' *Skipper's Guide* for up-to-date information and licence fees.

Public Cruising

Public cruises are available on trip boats and restaurant barges along the canal. At the time of writing there were five boats, the *Gipsy Princess, Janet Telford, Yarrow Seagull, Nolly Barge* and *Caledonian*. See Appendix 5 for contact details.

Gipsy Princess and *Janet Telford* are run by the Forth and Clyde Canal Society. *Gipsy Princess* is a 13m. (46ft) long, 36-seater cruiser with cabin and open deck accommodation, small shop and WC. *Janet Telford* is a 12-seater cruiser, also with cabin and open deck passenger space. The Society gives public cruises at a large number of local galas along the canal and the boats are also available for private charter. Contact the Society or phone 0141 772 1620 for further details.

Yarrow Seagull is specially designed to take wheelchairs using a hydraulic lift. She is operated by the Seagull Trust, and is based at Southbank Road in Kirkintilloch. Built by the apprentices at Yarrows shipyard she is 13m. (46ft) long and has a full-length cabin with accommodation for twelve passengers including helpers, a galley and WC. Cruises are given free of charge to disabled groups. Contact the Seagull Trust or phone on 0141 777 7165 for further details.

Nolly Barge is run by a voluntary group in Possilpark. The boat is a 17m. (55ft) residential cruiser with bunks for 12 passengers and a living room, galley and WC including full provision for disabled passengers. She is based on the Glasgow Branch beside British Waterways' headquarters at the Old Basin, Hamiltonhill. Her role is to give residential cruises and day trips to community groups such as youth clubs, disabled groups and adult organisations. Contact 0141 336 7859 for details.

Caledonian is a 18m. (58ft) long barge adapted from one of the old Clyde ferries and is based at Glasgow Road Bridge, Kirkintilloch. She can carry up to 40 for sit down meals and has a certificate to carry up to 50 passengers. She caters for individuals and parties for dinners and lunches. A speciality is made of private parties and weddings. Contact Jim Ferguson on 07970 13153 or 01738 850 348 for further details.

Canoeing and Sailing

Various clubs use the canal for canoeing and individuals also 'paddle their own canoe'. The Cumbernauld and Kilsyth Kayak Club is based at Auchinstarry Basin and runs summer outings and winter pool events. Contact Colin Scott on 01236 728844. Canoeing, kayaking and sailing are organised at Firhill Basin by the Forth and Clyde Canal Community Project, based at Maryhill Community Central Hall. They also run other activities such as orienteering and environmental projects. Contact 0141 333 9886 or 0141 332 9115 for details. A canoe club is also based at the 'Stables', Glasgow Road Bridge, Kirkintilloch.

Walking and Cycling

The towpath gives 55km. (34 miles) of good walking and cycling right across Scotland's central belt. It offers a wide variety of landscapes from town to country. There is plenty to enjoy including canal structures, historical features and wildlife, illustrated in previous chapters. The towpath is generally at least 2m. (6ft) in width and has a firm quarry stone dust surface. Ordnance Survey 1:50,000 scale sheets 64 and 65 cover

Canoeing at Auchinstarry.

A cruiser using the canal to transit from sea to sea.

*The towpath, as here at Lambhill, is ideal for walking
and can be used by wheelchairs and pushchairs.*

Cycling is a popular recreation for all the family.

the route and more detailed 1:25,000 maps are also available. See also the maps and appendices in this *Guidebook* for further information.

Cyclists can obtain a free permit from British Waterways. The western section of the towpath from Clydebank to Bowling also forms part of the Glasgow to Loch Lomond cycleway. Having walkers and cyclists on the same track can lead to problems, but given mutual courtesy and respect these can be minimised. The towpath is intended for slow enjoyment of the countryside, not for fast cycling. Walkers can combine the towpath with many local footpaths to give circular walks and visits to places of interest. Some ideas are:

Bowling to Temple: 12.8km. (8 miles) one way.
This walk gives a good appreciation of the many faces of the canal and takes advantage of the railway line which runs close by for the return journeys. Features include the Bowling sea lock and boat filled marina, wildlife area at Old Kilpatrick, the completely new stretch of canal beyond Great Western Road, Cloberhill Lock flight and the welcoming pubs at journey's end at Temple.

Glasgow Branch and the River Kelvin: 11.2km. (7 miles) circular.
This walk takes in the canal's most impressive structures and passes through one of its one time industrial heartlands. Following the start at Temple, features include the magnificent Kelvin Aqueduct followed by the striking Maryhill Locks with their oval basins. Glasgow branch features include Firhill Basin, Hamiltonhill Basin and the impressive Spiers Wharf buildings. Return is by the very pleasant River Kelvin Walkway which requires some street walking or bus to Kelvingrove, and there is a steep climb up from the walkway to the canal at the aqueduct.

Bishopbriggs to Kirkintilloch: 12.8km. (8 miles) there and back.
The walk starts at the Leisuredrome, passes through the beautiful Cadder Woods, sees plenty of big boat activity centred on the 'Stables' and finishes at Kirkintilloch with the old slipway, new Yarrow Seagull boathouse and restored town centre bridge. Several buses travel between Kirkintilloch and Bishopbriggs if required. Alternative routes include a visit to the River Kelvin at Cadder and a walk down to Possil Loch wildlife reserve.

Twechar to Craigmarloch: 9.6km. (6 miles) circular.
Starting at the restored Twechar lifting bridge this walk takes in a beautiful winding treelined section to Auchinstarry Basin, and another lovely treelined section to Craigmarloch. Craigmarloch was the destination of many of the old 'Queen' cruises and the old stables can also be seen just north along the main canal feeder lade. The return walk is via the Antonine wall over the tops of Croy Hill and Bar Hill, giving extensive views over the Forth and Clyde valley. The remains of the Roman ditch and of Bar Hill Fort are clearly visible. Alternative routes include a return from Auchinstarry to Twechar via Auchinstarry Loch and the River Kelvin Walkway, and walks from Craigmarloch up to Colzium Estate and Banton Loch.

Craigmarloch to Wyndford: 11.2km. (7 miles) circular.
This walk takes in the old basins, lade and stables at Craigmarloch, the Dullatur Bog wildlife reserve, the broadest reach on the canal and Wyndford Lock at the far-eastern end of the summit reach. The return walk is via the minor road south to the Antonine

Wall, and then the route of the wall and minor roads back to Craigmarloch. An alternative circular route leaves the canal at Kelvinhead, to Banton Village and then return via Banton Loch and minor roads.

Bonnybridge to Camelon: 11.2km. (7 miles) circular.
Starting at the new lift bridge at Bonnybridge, this walk gives a very pleasant towpath walk to the magnificent new 'Falkirk Wheel' boat lift at the new entrance to the Union Canal and on to Lock 16, which is the beginning of the Camelon lock flight. Along the way there are some magnificent views of the Ochil Hills to the north. Return via the Antonine Wall including the superbly preserved section of Roman ditch at Watling Lodge and the best preserved Roman fort at Rough Castle. By starting the return journey at the Falkirk Wheel the walk can be shortened by 3.2km. (2 miles). As a pleasant shorter alternative, walk west from Bonnybridge to Underwood Lockhouse. Halfway along this route a pend beneath the canal gives access to Seabegs Wood with a well-preserved section of Antonine wall and ditch.

The Antonine Wall

The Roman Antonine Wall runs close to the canal along much of its length and features in many of the suggested walks. It was built about AD 143 on the instruction of the Emperor Antoninus Pius across the narrowest neck of Scotland. It covers a distance of 60km. (37 miles), from Bo'ness on the Forth to Old Kilpatrick on the Clyde and

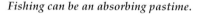
Fishing can be an absorbing pastime.

was made of turves and clay blocks on a stone base about 4.5m. (15ft) wide. The height of the rampart is not known but it could well have reached 3m. to 3.5m. (10 to 12ft), possibly topped with a walkway and wattle breastwork. A ditch was excavated in front of this wall, originally up to 12m. (40 f0t) wide and 3.9m. (13ft) deep.

Several major forts were built along the wall, together with small mile fortlets. A military way was built behind the wall, with a cambered surface some 4.8m. (16ft) wide. Very little remains of the turf wall but the ditch is very clear for long stretches between Falkirk and Twechar, particularly near Lock 16 at Camelon and over Bar Hill and Croy Hill near Kilsyth. The remains of two forts, Rough Castle near Falkirk and Bar Hill near Twechar, are still visible along this stretch of wall.

At its peak strength the Wall was garrisoned by up to 7,000 men, some from as far away as Syria. It was used as a base for forays to the north, with forts maintained up to the Tay. The tribes behind the Wall settled down to a prosperous existence under the *Pax Romana*. They started to build substantial stone houses, develop agriculture to feed the troops, and trades such as pottery, mining and smithying flourished. Along the Wall itself the troops brought coriander and poppy seed to flavour their bread. When the old well was excavated in the Bar Hill Fort early in the twentieth century leather shoes were found, together with iron weapons and tools, bronze ornaments, animal bones, shells and coins. They even found the pulley wheel and well bucket! The settled life of the soldiers and the citizenry was not to last. The Wall was briefly abandoned around AD 158 and finally abandoned about AD 163, only twenty years after construction. Thereafter the Romans retired to Hadrian's Wall and tried to control the northern tribes by patrols and by treaties.

Fishing

The canal has some of the best coarse fishing in Scotland. Its deep slow-moving water, with plenty of weed for cover, gives good breeding grounds for the perch and roach that have been established in the canal for many years. In more recent years tench, carp and bream, introduced by anglers, have been spreading successfully, particularly in the eastern half of the summit reach, between Wyndford and Kirkintilloch. Spring and summer are best for canal fishing, during winter the cold water tends to make the fish very lethargic. Spawning is generally around May but can move into June if the spring is cold. Various clubs hold competitions with record catches of tench weighing more than 3kg. (7lb.), carp weighing 8kg. (18lb.), eels measuring over .75m. (2ft 6ins) and an amazing 63.5kg. (140lb.) shoal of roach caught by fourteen anglers at one competition.

The canal's biggest predator is the pike, providing sport for pike fishermen over the winter months in particular. Giants weighing more than 11kg. (25lb.) have been caught in the canal. Most of these are put back to live and fight another day. Fishing permits can be purchased from British Waterways costing £5.85 in 2001.

Please remember a few don'ts. Don't light fires, leave litter, use lead weights or leave abandoned line as this causes havoc with the water birds.

Pubs and Restaurants

Whether you are boating or walking, cycling or fishing, it is always a pleasure to enjoy a drink or a meal beside the canal. In the last few years several new very popular establishments have opened:

'The Glen Lusset': Near Erskine Bridge. Beer Garden faces canal.

'Debra Rose': Clydebank. The 'Chip Ship' takeaway and restaurant.

'The Canal': Temple. Restaurant and pub; own microbrewery.

'Lock 27': Temple, next to Bearsden Road Bridge. Bar snacks and meals. Picnic tables by canal.

'Kelvin Dock': Maryhill, across main road; small library and old canal pictures in bar.

'The Stables': Glasgow Road Bridge, near Kirkintilloch. Bar snacks and meals. Picnic tables by canal. Historic building.

'Lock, Stock & Barrel': Twechar, south from bridge. Bar snacks. Traditional beers.

'Underwood Lockhouse': Lock 17, near Bonnybridge. Licensed Indian Restaurant and bar. Picnic tables by canal. Historic building.

'Falkirk Wheel': Visitor centre.

'Union Inn': Lock 16, Camelon. Bar snacks and meals. Historic building, known locally as 'Auntie Kates'.

'Canal Inn': Lock 15, Camelon. Pub known locally as 'The War Office' since its days as HQ of the Camelon Home Guard.

'Rosebank': Camelon Road, Falkirk. Beefeater restaurant and bar. Bar snacks and meals. Historic building.

Lock 27 at Temple, one of a number of popular pub/restaurants.

The Stables, a well frequented pub/restaurant near Kirkintilloch.

Join a Canal Society

Joining a Canal Society is probably the best 'What to do' recommendation we can make. This way you can keep up to date with what is happening and play a part in the revival of the canal. The three main Societies are the Forth & Clyde Canal Society, the Falkirk & District Canals Society and the Scottish Inland Waterways Association.

The Forth & Clyde Canal Society operates the *Gipsy Princess* and *Janet Telford*. The Society holds meetings, walks, clean ups and cruises. It acts as a political ginger group to improve the canal and had a major input to the Millennium Link. Our journal is the *Canal News*. Falkirk & District Canals Society campaigns for the Union and Forth & Clyde Canals in the Falkirk area. Scottish Inland Waterways Association is the umbrella group for all the local canal societies in Scotland. Further details of the Forth & Clyde Canal Society are given towards the end of this Guide and contact addresses for all the Societies are given in Appendix 5.

Looking After The Canal

The canal is a publicly owned asset, operated and managed by British Waterways. It is their task to maintain the fabric of the canal, ensure adequate water supplies and provide for the many uses the facility is put to.

British Waterways

Inland waterways in Britain were nationalised under the Transport Act of 1947 and placed under the control of the British Transport Commission. This, in turn, was abolished by the Transport Act of 1962 and replaced by the British Waterways Board (BWB) on 1 January 1963.

BWB made detailed studies on the condition and potential use of waterways through the mid-1960s and reports on these led to a Government White Paper in 1967 entitled *British Waterways: Recreation and Amenity*. It was followed by the Transport Act of 1968 which classified the waterways according to their principal use at that time. Those waterways used principally for the carriage of commercial freight were classified as 'Commercial Waterways', while those used principally for cruising, fishing and other recreational purposes were classified as 'Cruising Waterways'. The remaining, mainly disused, canals were left unclassified and described by the Act as 'Remainder Waterways'. BWB had to maintain the waterways to an appropriate level for their classification; in Scotland the Caledonian and Crinan Canals were 'Commercial Waterways', all the others were 'Remainder Waterways'. The Forth & Clyde and Union Canals suffered from the minimal maintenance their status attracted, but the Millennium Link has changed all that.

The word 'Board' was dropped from the BWB title in 1988 and the organisation became known as British Waterways (BW). The management structure was reorganised to move the decision making process closer to the ground; six Regions, with subsidiary waterway units, were created.

Signs are useful if the towpath is to be shared safely by many users.

Being a nationalised undertaking, BW receives Government funding. This comes from two sources, because under the devolution settlement, responsibility for Scotland's inland waterways was transferred to the Scottish Executive in Edinburgh. BW is therefore answerable to two government ministers in two parliaments for the money it spends. Special arrangements have been made in Scotland to develop and maintain contacts with the Scottish Executive.

The ability to raise funds for the development of the social, environmental and economic potential of waterways was enhanced in 1999 when a new organisation, the Waterways Trust, was set up. The Trust, which is separate from BW, seeks to establish partnerships and secure funding to promote greater public enjoyment and awareness of Britain's waterways. The Trust's Scottish team is based at BWs Applecross Street offices in Glasgow.

Management and Maintenance

In Scotland, the management unit 'Lowland Canals' was set up to manage the Forth & Clyde, Union and Monkland Canals. The Waterway Manager's team is made up of people who look after Engineering, Estates, Commercial Development, Recreational Development, Finance and Regeneration. They are based at Falkirk in Rosebank House, part of a 'Beefeater' pub/restaurant development in an old bonded warehouse beside the Forth & Clyde Canal at Camelon Bridge.

Overall Scottish affairs are handled from the Regional Office at Applecross Street, Glasgow. The team is led by the Regional Director supported by a core of expert staff who provide Engineering, Estates, Commercial and Financial advice. The Partnership Department is also based at Applecross Street.

The Waterway Supervisors provide first line management of the direct labour waterway staff. The Engineering Supervisor provides on the spot service on relevant matters as do the Waterway Administrator and Secretary/Clerk. Daily maintenance is carried out by a team of operatives who have to be versatile and 'multi-skilled'. Their range of routine tasks include painting, pointing, repairing fences and walls, cleaning ditches, clearing scrub, removal of rubbish, maintaining weirs and sluices, and, in winter, salting bridges and catwalks to comply with statutory safety requirements. The reopened canal has of course added operational functions, like working locks and bridges.

Vandalism is a continual source of unwanted problems and much time and effort is wasted by the continual need to combat its effects.

Water Supply

It may seem obvious, but the canal needs water. It comes from reservoirs and natural water courses and, contrary to popular misconception, the water is not stagnant, it flows constantly. And it is BW's task to ensure that the flow is maintained, that the canal level remains constant and the structures associated with water supply and control are maintained. A sizeable amount of the time and money spent on the

Opposite: *Maintenance of historic structures like the Kelvin Aqueduct is a vital part of British Waterways role.*

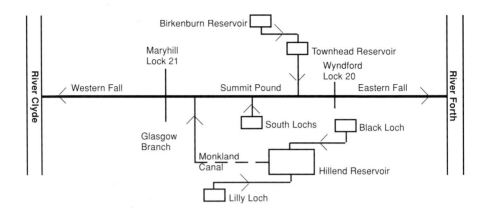

waterway goes into care, maintenance and improvement of the water supply. The amount of time this can take is illustrated by the one and half hour uphill trek, on foot, needed to reach one of the reservoirs for inspection, and if a repair job has to be done it can be very time consuming.

The principal reservoirs are near Kilsyth. Birkenburn Reservoir, high in the hills behind the town feeds water to the Townhead Reservoir, to the east of the town at the base of the hills, and from there the water is fed by a lade into the canal at Craigmarloch. This supply is augmented at the western end of the summit by water

The outfall from the great Hillend Reservoir at Caldercruix.

Keeping the channel dredged for boats is an essential element of canal maintenance.

from the Monkland Canal. Although this canal was closed in the 1950s and much of it was filled in, a pipeline was laid to maintain the water flow. The system starts with two small reservoirs, the Black Loch and Lilly Loch which feed into the huge Hillend Reservoir at Caldercruix; the largest man-made body of water when it was created in the 1790s. The water is fed from there into the North Calder Water and taken out into the Monkland system at Woodhall, Calderbank. It enters the canal basins at Port Dundas. A third major system can feed water from the Bothlin Burn at Craigenbay, Lenzie to the canal at Kirkintilloch. Historically the Union Canal also fed water into the Forth & Clyde at Falkirk and this can be reinstated by the Millennium Link. Additionally a number of smaller water courses, land drainage, and water simply running off surrounding land, help to fill the canal.

This land drainage function has, if anything, increased over the years as more and more of the country is covered in tarmac. Run-off water entering the canal can be controlled before being released into appropriate rivers and streams, making the canal an essential part of central Scotland's land drainage and flood control system.

There are numerous level and flow recorders throughout the reservoir and feeder system, and along the canal. Canal and reservoir levels are read daily and about fifty flow rate readings are also recorded daily. A combination of team members' local knowledge and contact with other staff on the ground helps to ensure constant levels and flows.

Because water is a natural resource, natural forces can affect its supply. In wet weather water runs off adjacent land and creates an excess which has to be discharged to avoid stress on the canal structures. In such conditions the sluices from the reservoirs can be shut down and their excess discharged into rivers like the Kelvin and North Calder. Overflow weirs discharge excess water from the summit and other long pounds into natural water courses. In dry spells more water has to be released from the reservoirs to maintain canal levels.

Water flowing along the canal also has to be monitored and regulated. At locks the flow is regulated by setting the gate sluices to pass a volume of water, typically between 4.5 megalitres to a rare maximum of 63 megalitres (1 million to 14 million gallons) a day. It takes experience and know-how because it can be two days before the effect of a change in flow at Maryhill is apparent at Bowling. The closed lock gates can also act as weirs and because of their size small changes in level going over the gates can significantly affect the flow being passed downstream. Water is also moved by boats using the locks and care has to be taken by boaters to operate the locks in such a way as not to deplete the smaller pounds or to waste water. Some important locks are operated by BW staff to ensure that no mistakes are made which could affect the whole canal. Water is lost whenever a boat enters or leaves the canal at Bowling or Grangemouth and the sea-lock keepers have to inform the Waterway Supervisor on projected craft movements, so that instructions on the operation of sluices can be issued. Fluctuating water levels can inhibit boat movements.

Canal water can also be used by industry and the preservation of this function was seen as vital in the 1960s when the canal was closed to navigation. Although this use has diminished since then it is still one that BW has to consider in making water control arrangements. BW sees the use of the canal, as an aqueduct to move water to industrial users, as a potentially important source of revenue.

Capacity of Reservoirs

Reservoir	Million litres	Million gallons	Feeder
Birkenburn	695	153	Craigmarloch
Townhead	623	137	Craigmarloch
South Lochs	568	125	Bothlin Burn
Black Loch	796	175	Monkland Canal
Hillend	2,045	450	Monkland Canal
Lilly Loch	591	130	Monkland Canal

Using the Canal

The canal is used primarily as a recreational resource. For many years this has been limited to canoeing, fishing, walking and cycling while large boats have been confined to small sections. Restoration of navigation, however, means that these boats can now move anywhere on the canal, greatly enhancing BWs role in its daily management. Although many of the locks are operated by the boaters themselves, a few structures, like the Dalmuir Drop-lock, are operated by BW staff. Boaters can also request assistance either at the sea-locks or by contacting the Waterway Office at Falkirk.

It will take time for the full range of mooring and service facilities to be developed and so, for up-to-date information on these, boaters should consult the *Skipper's Guide* available from the offices in Falkirk and Glasgow. The offices will also provide information on passage and license fees, the income from which helps to maintain the fabric of the canal.

The ability to pass sea-going vessels makes the canal very special and helps to bring a sense of another world to inland places. It is anticipated that some 600 boats could use the canal for transit from coast to coast every year and that around 500 boaters can be encouraged to use the canal for permanent moorings. Canalside communities which had got used to a derelict waterway in their neighbourhood will now see boats either moored or passing through.

Community involvement is one of BWs most important functions and this is undertaken by the Partnership Team. It is vitally important that people living with the canal see it as enhancing their area and embrace it as their own. The Partnership Team therefore works with schools and colleges to involve young people and encourages them to undertake canal related projects. The Team also works with local groups, like housing associations, to explore ways in which they can benefit from the canal and perhaps also to become involved through links with groups like the Forth & Clyde Canal Society. Both BW and FCCS regard visiting local groups and giving talks as a valuable way of communicating with people and finding out what they want to get out of their canal.

These community links are also valued by the local authorities who see the Millennium Link as providing a catalyst for local businesses to expand and create jobs. The canal's restoration is seen as only the start of the project and it is hoped that in the first ten years after its completion around 4,000 jobs could have been created.

Towpath improvements as part of the Millennium Link project will help to enhance the canal as a traffic-free place to enjoy walking, running, cycling, fishing and other land-based activities. BW has to look after the path as assiduously as the water. The surface has to be kept in good order and with heavier use this maintenance function will increase. Stymie gates are placed at strategic places and access points to ensure that inappropriate towpath users, like scrambler bikes and all terrain vehicles, are kept off the path.

Perhaps the single most important aspect of the canal for land and water-based pursuits is the environment. The canal would be a dull place if all people could see was concrete and bricks, and it is one of BWs most important functions to preserve and manage the green corridor that the canal provides through town and country. The construction phase of the Millennium Link project inevitably disturbed vegetation and wildlife, although some aspects of the work also enhanced habitats and removed pollution. With the heavy work over, BW can concentrate on managing and developing the environmental resource in a way which will allow it to flourish for the enjoyment of all canal users for the foreseeable future.

Three 'generations' of British Waterways personnel have helped with this chapter. It was compiled for the first Guidebook *by Claire Lindsay, revised by Ian Law for the next and has now been updated from information supplied by Community Liaison Officer Andy Carroll. The Forth & Clyde Canal Society is indebted to them all.*

Appendix 1   Locks & Bridges

Name   Distance from Bowling

Name	KILOMETRES	MILES & YARDS	
Bowling Sea Lock 40	0.00	0	
Old Sea Lock 39	0.00	0	disused
Railway Bridge	0.16	170	
Bowling Bridge (38)	0.19	210	bascule
Bowling Lock 38	0.28	310	
Ferrydyke Bridge (37)	1.09	1,190	bascule
Dalnotter Lock 37	1.91	1 330	
Dalnotter Bridge (36)	2.11	1 550	swing bndge
Dalmuir West Bridge (35)	3.86	2 700	bascule
Dalmuir Drop-lock	4.49	2 1,390	also Dalmuir Bridge (34)
Trafalgar Street Footbridge	4.85	3 30	
Kilbowie Road Bridge (33)	6.15	3 1,450	
Sylvania Way Footbridges	6.21	3 1,510	two adjacent, opening bridges
Argyll Road Bridge	6.47	4 40	
Linnvale Footbridge (32)	7.66	4 1,340	bascule
Duntreath Avenue	8.04	4 1,750	
Boghouse Lower Lock 36	8.16	5 130	+ footbridge
Lock 35	8.47	5 460	+ footbridge
Blairdardie Lock 34	8.65	5 660	
Blairdardie Lock 33	8.81	5 840	
Bard Avenue Bridge (30)	9.09	5 1,140	bascule
Great Western Road	9.43	5 1,510	
Cloberhill Lock 32	9.89	6 260	+ footbridge
Cloberbill Lock 31	9.99	6 370	
Cloberhill Lock 30	10.34	6 750	
Cloberhill Lock 29	10.44	6 860	
Cloberhill Lock 28	10.54	6 970	
Westerton Footbridge	11.05	6 1,530	
Netherton Bridge (28)	11.90	7 700	swing bridge
Lynch Estate Bridge	12.34	7 1,180	
Temple Bridge (27)	12.52	7 1,370	
Temple Lock 27	12.59	7 1,450	+ footbridge
Temple Lock 26	12.77	7 1,650	
Govan Cottage Bridge (26)	13.37	8 550	
Maryhill Lock 25	13.98	8 1,210	
Maryhill Lock 24	14.03	8 1,270	
Maryhill Lock 23	14.08	8 1,320	

	KILOMETRES	MILES & YARDS	
Maryhill Lock 22	14.16	8	1,410	
Maryhill Lock 21	14.22	8	1,470	+ footbridge
Glasgow Branch enters	15.07	9	640	
Lambhill Bridge (19)	16.69	10	660	
Farm Bridge (18)	19.95	12	700	
Cadder Bridge (17)	21.22	13	330	
Hungryside Bridge (16)	22.49	13	1,720	
Glasgow Road Bridge (15)	23.77	14	1,360	
Townhead Bridge (13)	26.06	16	350	
Nicolson Bridge	26.25	16	550	
Hillhead Bridge (12)	26.59	16	920	swing bridge
Water Pipe	27.79	17	480	
Twechar Bridge (11)	31.51	19	1,030	lifting bridge
Auchinstarry Bridge (10)	34.30	21	560	
Craigmarloch Bridge (9)	36.10	22	770	
Wyndford Lock 20	40.24	25	20	
Wyndford Bridge (8)	40.26	25	40	
A 80 Bridge	41.50	25	1,400	
Castlecary Bridge (7)	41.75	25	1,670	
Castlecary Lock 19	42.00	26	180	
Underwood Lock 18	42.46	26	680	+ footbridge
Underwood Lock 17	43.41	26	1,720	+ footbridge
Bonnybridge Bridge (6)	45.60	28	600	lifting bridge
The Falkirk Wheel	48.93	30	730	swing footbridge
Lock 16 and Bridge (5)	50.32	31	480	
Canal Street Lock 15	50.46	31	640	
Glenfuir Road Lock 14	50.67	31	860	+ footbridge
Lock 13	50.78	31	990	
Lock 12	50.90	31	1,120	
Lock 11	51.01	31	1,240	
Camelon Bridge (4)	51.07	31	1,300	
Lock 10	51.25	31	1,500	
Lock 9	51.42	31	1,690	
Railway Bridge	51.44	31	1,710	
Merers Bridge Lock 8	51.59	32	110	
Merchiston Lock 7	51.73	32	260	
Grahamston Lock 6	52.16	32	730	
Lock 5	52.62	32	1,240	
Bainsford Bridge (3)	52.66	32	1,280	
Abbotshaugh Lock 4	53.62	33	570	+ footbridge
Falkirk Distributor Road	54.32	33	1,340	new bridge
Lock 3	54.71	34	0	+ footbridge
Lock 2 Sea Lock	55.13	34	460	
Grangemouth	56.70	35	420	distance on old line
				to former Carron entrance

Locks and Bridges

1   Lock operation
    Carron Sea Lock, Dalmuir Drop-lock, Bowling Sea Lock all operated by BW staff.
    Locks 3 to 16, 20 and 21 customer operated with BW assistance.
    All other locks operated by customer

2   Bridge operation
    Bonnybridge lift bridge, Twechar lift bridge, Hillhead swing bridge, Sylvania Way
    opening bridges and Ferry Road (Dalnottar) swing bridge are all operated by BW
    staff.
    Netherton swing bridge and five bascule bridges between locks 32 and 39 are
    customer operated with BW assistance. All other bridges fixed with 3m. (10ft)
    headroom.

3   Operating hours.
    The lowland canals operate seven days a week in spring, summer and autumn
    between the hours of 0800 and 2000. Winter hours are 0800 to 1600.

4   The locks are generally 20.9m. (68ft 6ins) long, 6m. (19ft 8in) wide, and have an
    average rise of 2.4m. (8ft).
    The Sea locks at Bowling and Grangemouth have larger dimensions and a rise
    approximately double that of the normal locks. Dalmuir Drop-lock is 67.83m. (225ft
    6ins) long altogether and the central bridge section is 19.83m. (65ft) long between
    the barriers.

5   Distances are based on the *Table of Distances* published in 1912 by the Caledonian
    Railway Company) modified to take account of changes since then. They should
    not be taken as absolutely accurate and metric conversions have been rounded.

6   The following bridges are on the Glasgow Branch
    Ruchill Bridge (20)
    Murano Street Village Footbridge (20A)
    Firhill Bridge (21)
    Rockvilla Bridge (22) Footbridge (Bascule, BW operated)
    Ann Street (23) Culverted infill section
    Port Dundas (24) Culverted inflll section

    There are no locks on the Glasgow Branch.

    The width and headroom of Ruchill Bridge are non standard.

7   Original bridge numbers are given in brackets although some are not original
    structures.

8   See BW *Skipper's Guide* for up to date information.

Appendix 2   Boating Facilities

Trip Boats

Boat	Service	Phone
Gipsy Princess	Charters and Galas	0141 772 1620
Janet Telford	Charters and Galas	0141 772 1620
Yarrow Seagull	Disabled Groups	0141 777 7665
Nolly Barge	Residential Groups	0141 336 7859
Caledonian	Restaurant Barge	07970 13153

Canoeing and Sailing

Cumbernauld and Kilsyth Kayak Club	01236 728 844
Forth and Clyde Canal Community Project	0141 332 9886

Slipways, Landing Stages and Moorings

Camelon	Landing stage by Union Inn at Lock 16
Craigmarloch	Small steel landing stage close to bridge
Auchinstarry Basin	Concrete slipway suitable for trailable boats. Sheet pile landing stage. Large basin to be converted into a marina
Kirkintilloch	Hay's Slip, Southbank Road. Large original canal shipyard slipway.
The Stables	Glasgow Road Bridge. Large modern concrete slip with rail mounted boat trolley.
Bishopbriggs	Timber landing stage by Farm Bridge, across road from Leisuredrome.
Old Basin Works	BW headquarters on Glasgow Branch Rough slipway suitable for 4 wd vehicles.
Firhill Basin	Glasgow Branch. Hardcore slip suitable for small boats.
Maryhill	Sandbank Street. Small steep timber and concrete slipway.
Kelvin Dock	Old boatyard slip between Locks 22 and 23.
Moorings	Overnight moorings are available at Carron Sea Lock, Auchinstarry Basin and Bowling Basin, with water supply, showers etc. to be installed at time of writing.

Otherwise boats are able to moor alongside the towpath at a large number of locations, formal (e.g. The Stables) and informal.

British Waterways

Remember to contact BW on 0141 332 6936 or 01324 671217 for:

Licences	Transit licences, term licences, marina licences, inland licences, trailer boat licences and small craft licences are all available. Contact BW for up-to-date prices.
Booking	Where BW staff assistance is required for locks and bridges.
Skipper's Guide	The current BW *Skipper's Guide* will update the information given in this Appendix and give more detailed information. Phone or view on www.scottishcanals.co.uk.
Permits	Permits for casual users of small, unpowered craft such as canoes and rowing boats are available free of charge from BW.

Appendix 3   Historic Buildings

Listed Buildings

NAME	DATE LISTED	CATEGORY
1. Two canal drawbridges at Bowling	1973	B
2. Bowling Basin Swing Bridge	24/4/1991	B
3. Bowling lower canal basin & entrance	24/4/1991	B
4. Bowling upper canal basin & lock	24/4/1991	B
5. Bowling upper canal basin: lock-keeper's houses	24/41991	B
6. Custom House, Bowling	9/5/1993	B
7. Bilsland Drive Aqueduct	6/4/1992	B
8. Forth and Clyde Canal Aqueduct adjoing Skaethorn Road Bridge	10/7/1989	A
9. 11, 23, 25 & 29 Canal Bank, with bank openings	6/4/1992	B
10. 2 Spiers Wharf, Canal House	15/12/1970	B
11. Forth and Clyde Canal Applecross Street	13/3/1997	B
12. 5–7 Applecross Street. Former canal lock-keeper's house	17/2/1992	C(S)
13. Forth and Clyde Canal Aqueduct Maryhill Road	10/7/1989	B
14. Midwharf Street, North Canalbank Street and North Spiers Wharf: bascule bridge including stone platforms/abutments.	17/2/1992	B
15. Midwharf Street, North Canalbank Street and North Spiers Wharf: swing bridge including stone platforms and revetments.	17/2/1992	B
16. Cadder Bridge Cottages	17/8/1997	B
17. Canal buildings at Glasgow Bridge, near Bishopbriggs.	5/8/1974	B
18. Luggie Bridge, High Street, Kirkintilloch	14/5/1971	B
19. Luggie Water Aqueduct & Bridge	29/4/1986	A
20. 22 & 24 Canal Street, Falkirk	23/4/1979	C(S)
21. Canal Inn, Canal Street, Falkirk	23/4/1979	C(S)
22. Cottage and Lock 11, Falkirk	23/4/1979	C(S)
23. Cottage at Lock 9, Falkirk	23/4/1979	C(S)
24. Red Lion Inn, Bankside, at Bainsford Bridge	23/4/1979	C(S)
25. Union Inn, Tamfourhill Road, Port Downie	21/3/1960	B

Scheduled Monuments on Forth & Clyde Canal

MONUMENT	CLASSIFICATION	MAP	GRID REF
Bowling Basin drawbridge	Industrial	64	NS451735
Ferrydyke drawbridge	Industrial	64	NS458730
Linnvale drawbridge	Industrial	64	NS511700
Bisland Drive Aqueduct	Industrial	64	NS575680
Aqueduct, Stockingfield Junction	Industrial	64	NS571689
Aqueduct, Possil Road	Industrial	64	NS558767
Bard Avenue drawbridge	Industrial	64	NS525697
Bascule Bridge, Port Dundas	Industrial	64	NS592666
Maryhill Graving Dock	Industrial	64	NS562690
& five locks			NS565689
Maryhill Road Aqueduct	Industrial	64	NS567688
Old Basin, Applecross Street	Industrial	64	NS585672
Overflow & Railway Tunnel	Industrial	64	NS572685
River Kelvin Aqueduct	Industrial	64	NS561689
Locks 9 to 16	Industrial	64	NS868800
			NS878805

The Union Inn, built in the 1820s
to cater for people travelling by canal between Glasgow and Edinburgh.

Appendix 4   How to get there

By Road

East from Glasgow. The A803 stays within 1.6km. (1 mile) of the canal from Bishopbriggs to Falkirk. Side roads give access to the canal at regular intervals.

Within Glasgow. The Cowcaddens Road/Garscube Road/Maryhill Road thoroughfare follows the Glasgow Branch of the canal closely from Port Dundas to Maryhill Locks, with regular access points.

West from Glasgow. The A82 stays within 1.6km. (1 mile) of the canal from Anniesland to Clydebank, and numerous side roads give access. From Clydebank to Bowling the A814 (Dumbarton Road) stays within .4km. (.25 mile) of the canal throughout.

By Rail

East from Glasgow. A half hourly Glasgow Queen Street to Stirling/Dunblane service operates to stations at Bishopbriggs, Lenzie and Croy, also certain express trains between Glasgow Queen Street and Edinburgh Waverley stop at Croy. Falkirk Grahamston station is served by the half hourly Glasgow Queen Street High Level service, which operates via Cumbernauld.
Falkirk Grahamston Station lies about .8km. (.5 mile) east of the canal, while Bishopbriggs, Lenzie and Croy stations are all just over 1.6km. (1 mile) to the south of it.

West from Glasgow. Trains from Glasgow Queen Street Low Level and Glasgow Central Low Level stations serve the following stations, all situated close to the canal: Anniesland, Westerton, Drumchapel, Drumry, Singer, Clydebank, Dalmuir, Kilpatrick and Bowling. Clydebank is situated on a separate loop from Anniesland, Westerton, Drumchapel, Drumry and Singer. The two loops come together at Dalmuir.
For more information pick up a local timetable at any station or contact the:
National Rail Enquiry Service 0845 7 48 49 50
Minicom 0845 60 50 600
Website: www.scotrail.co.uk

By Bus

East from Glasgow. First Edinburgh run services between Glasgow Buchanan Street Bus Station and Falkirk. Service 27 is particularly useful: it passes close to the Canal at Cadder near Bishopbriggs, Glasgow Bridge near Kirkintilloch, Kirkintilloch, Kilsyth, Banknock, Bonnybridge and Camelon
First Glasgow run services between Glasgow and the Kirkintilloch area, their service 184 Glasgow Kilsyth, is very useful: it passes close to the canal at Cadder, Glasgow Bridge, Kirkintilloch, Twechar and Auchinstarry.

Within Glasgow. First Glasgow run numerous services which cross or pass near the canal. Service 61 from Hope Street in the City Centre runs along Maryhill Road, conveniently serving the Glasgow Branch of the canal.

West of Glasgow. First Glasgow run several services in the vicinity of the canal
For more details of bus services contact:
Buchanan Street Bus Station 0141 333 3708
Traveline 0870 608 2608
Strathclyde Passenger Transport 0141 332 7133
First Glasgow 0141 636 3195
Website: www.firstglasgow.co.uk

Appendix 5   Useful contacts

British Waterways
Canal House
1 Applecross Street
Glasgow
G4 9SP
Tel: 0141 332 6936
Website:
www.britishwaterways.co.uk

Scottish Canals
Canal House
1 Applecross Street
Glasgow
G4 9SP
Tel: 0141 332 6936
Website:
www.scottishcanals.co.uk

Forth & Clyde Canal Society
Nancy Lawton
101 Kirkintilloch Road
Bishopbriggs
G64 2AA
Tel: 0141 772 1620
Website:
www.forthandclyde.org.uk

Falkirk & District Canals Society
May MacIntyre
196 Glasgow Road
Camelon
Falkirk
FK1 4JA
Tel: 01324 622997

Paisley Canal & Waterway Society
19 Greenhill Crescent
Elderslie
Renfrewshire
PA5 9AW

Scottish Inland Waterways Association
1 Craiglockhart Crescent
Edinburgh
EH14 1DZ
Tel: 0131 443 2533

Forth & Clyde Canal Community Project
Laura Bowden
Community Central Hall
204 Maryhill Road
Glasgow
G20 7YE
Tel: 0141 333 9886

Seagull Trust
Princes House
5 Shandwick Place
Edinburgh
EH2 4RG
Tel: 0131 229 1789
Website:
www.seagulltrust.org.uk

Gipsy Princess
Nancy Lawton
101 Kirkintilloch Road
Bishopbriggs
G64 2AA
Tel: 0141 772 1620
Website:
www.forthandclyde.org.uk

Janet Telford
Nancy Lawton
101 Kirkintilloch Road
Bishopbriggs
G64 2AA
Tel: 0141 772 1620
Website:
www.forthandclyde.org.uk

Yarrow Seagull
David McPherson
17 Woodilee Cottages
Lenzie
Kirkintilloch
G66 3UA
Tel: 0141 777 7165
Website:
www.seagulltrust.co.uk

Nolly Barge
Mags Harwood
Nolly Barge Project
Ground Flat C
187 Westercommon Road,
Glasgow
G22 5NE
Tel: 0141 336 7859

The Caledonian
Mr J. Ferguson
Caledonian Cruising
Balmerino
Perth Road
Abernethy
PH2 9LW
Tel: 01738 850348
07970 131535

East Dunbartonshire Libraries
Libraries Manager
Elizabeth Brown
Library Headquarters
2–4 West High Street
Kirkintilloch
G66 1AD
Tel: 0141 776 5666
Website:
www.eastdunbarton.gov.uk

Reference & Information Librarian
Don Martin
The William Patrick Library
2–4 West High Street
Kirkintilloch
G66 1AD
Tel: 0141 776 8090
Website:
www.eastdunbarton.gov.uk

East Dunbartonshire Museums
Cecilia McDaid
Curator
The Auld Kirk Museum
The Cross
Kirkintilloch
Tel: 0141 578 0144
Website:
www.eastdunbarton.gov.uk

Forth & Clyde Canal Guidebook
Editor
Paul Carter
'Woodlyn'
High Banton
Kilsyth
Tel: 01236 822437

(Enquiries, comments, and suggested additions for the next edition are welcome, and should be addressed to the editor at the above address. Enquiries regarding availability of the *Guidebook* should be addressed to East Dunbartonshire Libraries at the address opposite).

Bibliography

Books & Pamphlets

Aitken, James, & Co.   *'Fairy Queen' route illustrated guide* (1897). 40pp. illus. Kirkintilloch: James Aitken & Co.

Aitken, James, & Co.   *The famed Fairy Queen route: illustrated guide* (1916). 32pp. illus. Kirkintilloch: James Aitken & Co.

Aitken, James, & Co.   *Illustrated guide to 'Queen' steamers route* (nd). 32pp. illus. Kirkintilloch: James Aitken & Co. Aitken produced numerous editions of their informative little guidebook to the Port Dundas–Craigmarloch pleasure sailing route. Of which the above are just three examples.

Allan, John K.   *Their is a Cannal* (1977). 32pp. illus. maps. table. Falkirk: Falkirk Museums. A brief history of canal transport in the Falkirk area, covering both the Forth & Clyde and the Union Canal.

Anon.   *A companion for canal passengers betwixt Edinburgh and Glasgow* (1823). 36pp. Edinburgh: John Aitken. Mile by mile guide to the Union and Forth & Clyde canals. A reprint was published by the Linlithgow Union Canal Society in 1981.

Bailey, Geoff   *Locks, Stocks and Bodies in Barrels: a history of the canals in the Falkirk area* (2000). Falkirk: Falkirk Council Library Services. 23pp. illus. map. table. Deals with the Forth & Clyde and Union canals.

Bowman, A. Ian   *Kirkintilloch Shipbuilding* (1983). 83pp. illus. plans. tables. Bishopbriggs: Strathkelvin District Libraries. Concerned largely with puffer building, but also highlights some international shipbuilding at a Forth & Clyde Canal location.

Bowman, A. Ian   *Swifts & Queens: passenger transport on the Forth & Clyde Canal* (1984). 80pp. illus. map. diagrams. tables. Bishopbriggs: Strathkelvin District Libraries. A comprehensive survey, from the earliest services of the 1780s right down to the 1980s.

Bowman, A. Ian   *Symington and the Charlotte Dundas* (1981). 29pp. illus. diagrams. chronology. Falkirk: Falkirk Museums. Devoted to a Forth & Clyde Canal topic of world-wide significance: the first practical steamboats.

Bowman, A. Ian   *The Gipsy o' Kirky: S.S. Gipsy Queen* (1987). 32pp. illus. diagrams. Bishopbriggs: Strathkelvin District Libraries. An entire book devoted to the Canal's best remembered vessel.

Brown, Hamish	*Exploring the Edinburgh to Glasgow Canals (1997)* 106pp. illus. maps. Edinburgh: The Stationery Office. A well-illustrated guidebook to the environment of the Forth & Clyde and Union canals.
Crawford, J. Law	*Forth & Clyde Ship Canal in relation to the development of commerce* (1891). 108pp. fold. map. tables. diagrams. Glasgow: MacLaren & Sons. One of the most comprehensive accounts of a proposal that was under serious consideration at one time: a ship canal along the Forth & Clyde route.
Fairbairn, William	*Remarks on canal navigation* (1831). 93pp. London: Longman. Includes information about the experimental vessels that were being tried on the Forth & Clyde and other Scottish canals at the period. The illustrations include several Forth & Clyde boats.
Findlay, Bill	*Canal Seasons: Kirkintilloch–Bishopbriggs* (2001). 24pp. Kirkintilloch: East Dunbartonshire Council. Voyages on the *Yarrow Seagull* during spring, summer and autumn.
Fleming, G., ed.	*The Millennium Link: the rehabilitation of the Forth & Clyde and Union canals* (2000). 166pp. illus. maps. drawings. London: Thomas Telford Publishing. Papers presented at a conference organised by The Institution of Civil Engineers, Edinburgh, 29 June–1 July 2000.
Forrester, David	*The Great Canal that linked Edinburgh, Glasgow and London: a study of the finance and administration of the Forth & Clyde Navigation 1768–1816 A.D., with the first public accounts for 1815 A.D.* (1978; Second ed. 1980). 31pp. diagram. tables. bibliog. Glasgow: Strathclyde Convergencies. A detailed academic paper.
Hadfield, Charles	*British Canals: an illustrated history.* Seventh rev. ed. (1984). 352pp. illus. maps. diagrams. bibliog. Newton Abbot: David & Charles. Includes many references to the Forth & Clyde Canal.
Harvey, W.S. & Downs-Rose, G.	*William Symington: inventor and engine builder* (1980) 203pp. illus. diagrams. bibliog. London: Northgate Publishing Co. Has chapters on 'The first *Charlotte Dundas*' (pp.117–126) and 'The second *Charlotte Dundas*' (pp.127–142)
Hopkirk, James	*Account of the Forth & Clyde Navigation, from its origin to the present time* (1816). 82pp. Glasgow. Developed from a description of the canal in Sir John Sinclair's *Statistical Account of Scotland* (1793), Vol.5. pp.585–591.
Hume, John R.	*The Forth & Clyde Canal* (1979). 13pp. illus. bibliog. Glasgow: University of Strathclyde. A brief history of the canal, prepared to accompany an exhibition.
Hutton, Guthrie	*A Forth and Clyde Canalbum* (1991) 52pp. illus. map. bibliog. Glasgow: Richard Stenlake. A well-annotated collection of photographs.

Hutton, Guthrie	*Forth and Clyde: the comeback canal* (1998) 48pp. illus. Ochiltree: Stenlake Publishing. A further well-chosen selection of photographs, similar to the *Canalbum* (above).
Lindsay, Jean	*The Canals of Scotland* (1968). 238pp. illus. maps. tables. Newton Abbot: David & Charles. Widely recognised as a competent standard work. Chapter 1 (pp.15–51) deals with the Forth & Clyde.
McDonald, Dan	*The Clyde Puffer* (1977). 48pp. illus. map. diagram. table. Newton Abbot: David & Charles. Includes details of many vessels built at yards on the Forth & Clyde Canal.
Martin, Don	*The Forth & Clyde Canal: a Kirkintilloch view* (1977; Second ed. 1985). 32pp. illus, map. bibliog. Bishopbriggs: Strathkelvin District Libraries. A brief history of the canal, from a Kirkintilloch point of view.
Paget-Tomlinson, Edward W.	*The Complete Book of Canal & River Navigations* (1978). 361pp. illus. maps. plans. diagrams. bibliog. Wolverhampton: Waine Research Publications. Includes a section on the Forth & Clyde.
Pratt, Edwin A.	*Scottish Canals and Waterways* (1922). xi, 299p. illus. maps. plans. diagrams. bibliog. London: Selwyn & Blount. Regarded as the standard work on the subject before publication of Jean Lindsay's book.
Priestley, Joseph	*Historical account of the navigable rivers, canals and railways throughout Great Britain* (1831). xii, 776pp. map. plan. London: Longman. Reprint published by Frank Cass in 1967.
Rankine, J. & Rankine, W.H.	*Biography of William Symington, Civil Engineer* (1862). 82pp. diagrams. Falkirk: A. Johnston. Includes many important extracts from contemporary documents.
Royal Commission on the Ancient and Historical Monuments of Scotland	*Stirlingshire: an inventory of the ancient monuments. Vol.2* (1963). 487pp. illus. maps. plans. diagrams. Edinburgh: HMSO. Description of the Forth & Clyde Canal on pp.436–438.
Skempton, A.W., ed.	*John Smeaton, FRS* (1981). 291pp. illus. map. facsim. port. London: Thomas Telford. Biographical information on the builder of the Forth & Clyde Canal.
Weaver, C.P. & Weaver, C.R.	*Steam on Canals* (1983). 96pp. illus. Newton Abbot: David & Charles. Has good coverage of Forth & Clyde Canal boats.

Articles

Bowman, A. Ian 'Steamers on the Forth & Clyde Canal', *Transport History*, Vol.11 (1980), pp.130–161.

Bowman, A. Ian 'Tracing the Charlotte', *Transport History*, Vol.8 (1977), pp.3–29.

Bowman, A. Ian 'Tracing the Charlotte – further notes', *Transport History*, Vol.8 (1977), pp.106–109.

Carr, Frank G.G. 'Scottish short cut for yachtsmen: guide and sailing directions for the Forth and Clyde Canal', *Yachting World and Power Craft* (1939). June 30 issue, pp.663–667 & July 7 issue, pp.15–19. Two-part article describing the Canal as it was just before the outbreak of World War II

Clark, Sylvia 'Flyboats and Firms: a pendant to Jean Lindsay's article Passenger Traffic on British Canals', *Transport History*, Vol.11 (1980), pp.13–24.

Forrester, D.A.R. 'Early canal company accounts: financial and accounting aspects of the Forth & Clyde Navigation, 1768–1816', *Accounting and Business Research*, Vol.10, No.37A (1980), pp.109–123.

Forrester, D.A.R. 'The Forth & Clyde Canal: some leaders in its early years', *Glasgow Chamber of Commerce Journal*, Vol.68 (1983), pp.393–397.

Jones, Jean 'James Hutton and the Forth & Clyde Canal', *Annals of Science*, Vol.39 (1982), pp.255–263. Includes some interesting information relating to the construction of the canal.

Lindsay, Jean 'Passenger traffic on British canals: the correspondence of William Houston, 1830–1835, *Transport History*, Vol.9 (1978), pp.204–216. An important source for the background history of the 'Swift' boats.

Lindsay, Jean 'Promotion of the Forth & Clyde Canal: Glasgow versus Edinburgh', *Transport History*, Vol.11 (1980), pp.3–12. Includes details of a rival Glasgow proposal for a canal of much smaller dimensions.

Lindsay, Jean 'Robert Mackell and the Forth & Clyde Canal', *Transport History*, Vol.1 (1968), pp.285–292.

Potter, Hugh 'From Clyde to Forth', *Waterways World* (1985). February issue, pp.56–59, and March issue, pp.42–45. Well-illustrated two-part article.

Robison, John 'Account of the malleable iron passage-boat, now plying on the Forth & Clyde Canal', *Edinburgh Philosophical Journal*, Vol.2 (1820), pp.222–224. A contemporary account of the famous *Vulcan*; accompanied by a set of sketch plans.

Ward, Ian 'Vandalism by order', *Motor Boat & Yachting* (1984), August issue, pp.107–110. An investigation of the 'sad fate' of the Forth & Clyde Canal.

Official Reports

Forth & Clyde Canal Local (Subject) Plan. Report of survey by Working Party. July 1979.

Forth & Clyde Canal Local (Subject) Plan. The main issues. Forth & Clyde Canal Working Party. January 1980.

Forth & Clyde Canal Local (Subject) Plan. Draft written statement. Forth & Clyde Canal Working Party. October 1980.

Forth & Clyde Canal Local Plan. Publicity & Consultation Statement. Falkirk District Council & Strathclyde Regional Council. April 1987.

Forth & Clyde Canal Local Plan. Written Statement. Strathclyde Regional Council & Falkirk District Council. New edition, February 1996.

Forth & Clyde Canal Local Plan. Monitoring Report, 1989. Strathclyde Regional Council, 1990.

Bishopbriggs Canal Study; for the Burgh of Bishopbriggs. William Gillespie and Associates, November 1971.

Forth & Clyde Canal Study; for the Corporation of the City of Glasgow. William Gillespie & Associates. November 1971.

Forth & Clyde Canal Study and Bishopbriggs Canal Study: Second Report for the Corporation of the City of Glasgow and the Burgh of Bishopbriggs. William Gillespie & Partners, March 1974.

Royal Commission on Canals and Waterways. Reports. 1906–1909

Other Sources

For two decades the Forth & Clyde Canal Society newsletter *Canal News* (*Forth & Clyde Canal News* until 1989) has faithfully chronicled events in and around the Canal. A full set of the newsletter, from the first issue of June 1980, can be consulted at the William Patrick Library, Kirkintilloch. Since the commencement of the Millennium Link project British Waterways has published a newsletter, *The Link*, providing graphic information about all the latest developments. Again, a full set, from the first issue back in 1995, can be seen at the William Patrick Library.

A vital source for the history of the Forth & Clyde Canal is the deposit of minutes and other documents of the canal company, available at the National Archives of Scotland (West Search Room), Charlotte Square, Edinburgh. Maps, deeds and other documents are also held by British Waterways at their offices in Applecross Street, Hamiltonhill, Glasgow. Useful materials are also held by Falkirk Museums at their History Research Centre in Callendar Park, by The Mitchell Library, Glasgow, and by East Dunbartonshire Libraries at the William Patrick Library, Kirkintilloch. A large collection of canal photographs is also kept at the William Patrick Library.

Up-to-date information on the Canal can be found on the Internet, notably on the British Waterways (Scotland) website, www.scottishcanals.co.uk, and on the Forth & Clyde Canal Society pages at www.forthandclyde.org.uk. East Dunbartonshire Libraries has contributed 500 Forth & Clyde Canal images to the Scottish Cultural Resources Access Network (SCRAN). Along with a range of other canal images these can be found on the SCRAN website, at www.scran.ac.uk. Full access can only be obtained at subscribing libraries and museums.

Acknowledgements

This book would not have happened without the hard work of East Dunbartonshire Libraries, the authors of the various chapters, and British Waterways Scotland.

Elizabeth Brown and Don Martin of East Dunbartonshire had the vision to see that this *Guidebook* was needed and the publishing skills to ensure its success. Don and his colleague Myra Woods have also done a superb job in selecting photographs and preparing Appendices 3, 4, 5 and the Bibliography.

Guthrie Hutton, Richard Davies and Donald Mackinnon are long term veterans of the battle for Scotland's canals with a century of campaigning between them. This experience lends great weight to their chapters describing the canal and the campaign for its restoration. The late Ian Bowman produced a number of fine canal history studies, along with his authoritative chapter in this guide.

British Waterways have not only given great assistance with this book, they have also reopened the canal! They have described how BW looks after the restored canal, and their environmental scientist Olivia Lassière revised the chapter on wildlife.

Thanks also to Lewis Hutton for preparing the maps. All photographs, unless where otherwise marked, are from the collections of Guthrie Hutton and East Dunbartonshire Libraries.

Paul Carter
Editor

British Waterways Scotland

Welcome to the
Lowland canals of Scotland

May 2001 signalled the historic reopening
of the Forth and Clyde Canal.
The unique Falkirk Wheel and Union Canal
are targeted for a spring 2002 opening.

Experience the ever changing landscape, the rich variety of
wildlife and the industrial heritage of the Lowland Canals.
Take a boat trip along their tranquil waters
or walk or cycle along the towpath.

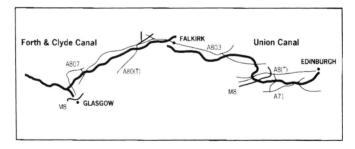

To find out more contact British Waterways Scotland's
Regional Office Telephone 0141 332 6936 and ask for the
Partnership Team or write to British Waterways Scotland,
Canal House, 1 Applecross Street Glasgow G4 9SP. You can
also try our web site: www.scottishcanals.co.uk

Restoring navigation was only the start:
the Forth & Clyde Canal Society's campaign
to reinstate the canal as a wonderful and successful,
local and national amenity goes on.
We care about the canal and want you to care too.

PLEASE JOIN US

Anyone can join and everyone is welcome.
You can take part in activities, or become a canal 'friend'
with your subscription. Our *newsletter* gives regular
information about what's going on.

We run boat trips, cruises and guided walks.
We give talks, hold members' meetings
and lobby those in authority.

For further information please contact:

The Membership Secretary,
101 Kirkintilloch Road,
Bishopbriggs,
Glasgow G64 2AA
tel: 0141 772 1620
www.forthandclyde.org.uk

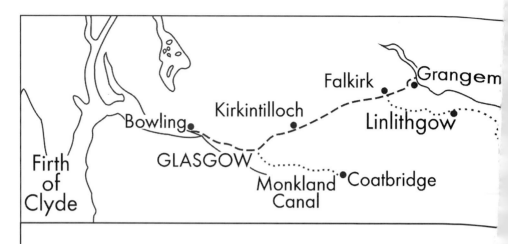

Forth & Clyde C

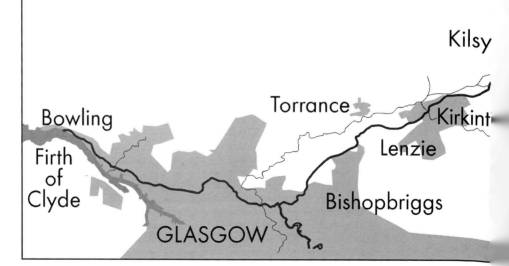